THE STEEL BAND GAME PLAN

Strategies for Starting, Building, and Maintaining Your Pan Program

Chris Tanner

Published in partnership with
MENC: The National Association for Music Education
Frances S. Ponick, Executive Editor

Rowman & Littlefield Education
Lanham • New York • Toronto • Plymouth, UK

Published in partnership with
MENC: The National Association for Music Education

Published in the United States of America
by Rowman & Littlefield Education
A Division of Rowman & Littlefield Publishers, Inc.
A wholly owned subsidiary of The Rowman & Littlefield Publishing
Group, Inc.
4501 Forbes Boulevard, Suite 200, Lanham, Maryland 20706
www.rowmaneducation.com

Estover Road
Plymouth PL6 7PY
United Kingdom

Photographs used with permission of Jeffrey A. Sabo

British Library Cataloguing in Publication Information Available

Library of Congress Cataloging-in-Publication Data

Tanner, Chris, 1970–
  The steel band game plan : strategies for starting, building, and
  maintaining your pan program / Chris Tanner.
    p. cm.
  Includes bibliographical references (p.   ) and discography (p.   ).
  ISBN-13: 978-1-57886-540-6 (hardcover : alk. paper)
  ISBN-10: 1-57886-540-9 (hardcover : alk. paper)
  ISBN-13: 978-1-57886-543-7 (pbk. : alk. paper)
  ISBN-10: 1-57886-543-3 (pbk. : alk. paper)
  1. Steel bands (Music)—Instruction and study. I. Title.
MT734.T36 2006
784.6'8—dc22   2006022925

CONTENTS

CONTENTS

FIGURES

FOREWORD

The steel band is a rapidly growing instrumental music class throughout school systems in the United States. I have witnessed this growth on a firsthand basis, as I am consistently getting invitations to conduct steel drum clinics and workshops for new programs, many in places far from major urban centers where I never imagined steel drums would find a home. It's always a curiosity as to how the directors, administrators, and principals of these new programs discovered this truly unique and exciting ensemble and implemented it into their music programs. After all, getting information about how to teach traditional band, orchestra, or chorus is relatively easy, as these types of ensembles have been around for a long time. But steel band? That's a different story. Compared to them, steel band is a relatively new instrumental class. Until now, only summer workshops, chat rooms, and the like have been available for quickie introductions and picking up information piecemeal, usually about how to learn it and rarely about how to teach it.

Now Chris Tanner, who has worked in the trenches as a director, composer, and teacher of steel band, brings us the text that has always been lacking to light. *The Steel Band Game Plan* is a primary resource, a comprehensive introduction written by a professional music educator for fellow professionals who want to expand their instrumental ensemble fields.

Compared to other ensembles, steel band is unique. Pans are not intimidating to the beginning student and are user-friendly instruments. I have witnessed pan build confidence in students unable to believe in their own musical as well as learning potential. An enthusiastic teacher can take a group of six or seven beginners and have them playing as an ensemble in about an hour with relative ease.

Steel band is suitable for a wide range of ages. I've seen third graders as well as adult beginners play well and happily. Everyone in the room, whether a listener or player, shares in the music together.

If you are interested in starting a steel band in your school, this book will be of great assistance to you. You'll find more details as you read on that will help clarify many questions you may have and fuel your fire for the exciting venture you are about to begin.

This is an exciting time for the steel drum world. It's growing exponentially in schools, communities, and homes. Students love the opportunity to move into making music quickly. As a music educator, you'll enjoy watching the joy it brings your students.

Chris's dedication and commitment to steel band make him the perfect candidate to write this book. He is an inspiration to students and teachers alike.

Tom Miller
International Steel Drum Artist and Clinician
Publisher, Pan Ramajay Productions

PREFACE: WHO SHOULD READ THIS BOOK?

Today, with so many steel bands operating in school environments, a need for appropriate pedagogical resources clearly exists. Until recently, the art form of steel band functioned as a small-time, grassroots movement. Most of the people directing steel bands had previously played in one, and so they had experience within the idiom. Knowledge was passed from person to person orally, in the tradition of many non-Western musical types.

However, a new crop of steel band directors has arisen. These individuals may have previous or concurrent experience in directing ensembles of a more traditional nature, such as wind band, orchestra, or choir. Nonetheless, they begin their tenure as a steel band director fundamentally unprepared for two important reasons. First, a novice director has likely had little or no exposure to steel band prior to taking the helm. These days, it is quite possible that new directors have never played in a steel band themselves, to say nothing of having had any exposure to pedagogy or teaching strategies. Second, the staple repertoire of steel bands primarily comprises Caribbean popular music, and these musical styles are not part of the normal listening experience of most outsiders (that is, people from outside the culture of the Caribbean). Thus, a new director who is not from the Caribbean typically begins his or her tenure without any knowledge of the repertoire.

I have written this book from an educator's perspective. In my own small corner of the world (southwest Ohio), there are fifteen steel band programs, and all but one are based in either secondary schools or universities. So it only makes sense to develop pedagogical materials that speak to the issues and challenges that educators face in developing their steel band programs. That being said, *any* steel band program can benefit from the strategies offered in this text. The issues and topics discussed herein are fundamental, and therefore apply to all steel band programs, regardless of the ensemble's setting or the director's background.

WHY DO STEEL BAND IN THE FIRST PLACE?

Let's face it: the undeniable popularity of steel band is spurring rapid growth. But why is the steel band so popular as an ensemble? A better question: is popularity alone enough to warrant pursuit of this potentially expensive activity in an educational environment where dollars are already stretched to their limit?

Without doubt, the Caribbean repertoire common to steel bands is a huge draw. People often want to become involved with steel band because of this music, and audiences love to hear steel bands perform it. People, particularly Westerners, find intrinsic value in the performance of Caribbean music; the rhythmic language of many Caribbean styles differs from our own, and that difference alone is worth exploring and experiencing. However, playing in a steel band yields greater, more significant benefits aside from merely enjoying a different musical vibe.

First, steel band can provide a welcoming entry point into a music program for the general population due to relative ease of technique. A completely inexperienced player can make an acceptable sound on a steel pan in less than one minute—there are no awkward fingerings to negotiate, no breathing control issues, no embouchures to learn. In short, almost anyone can have a baseline level of success playing in a steel band, and thus the ensemble provides a valuable resource for a music program that wants to reach out to as many as possible.

Second, a steel band is by and large a popular music ensemble; as such the performance practices are different from those of more traditional ensembles that perform art music primarily. For instance, members of a steel band must learn to groove with a rhythm section, as opposed to reacting to visual cues provided by a conductor. Additionally, the repertoire provides numerous opportunities for improvisation. As a result, the steel band can be a vehicle for introducing basic concepts of improvisation to the members. Furthermore, steel band personnel must learn to interact with audiences in the manner of other popular music ensembles; such interaction is quite distinct from the typical separation between performers and audience members in an art music context.

Finally, performers can explore both contemporary and past perspectives on the music-culture of Trinidad, the birthplace of steel drum instruments. The story of how steel pans came to be encompasses many disciplines: geography, history, anthropology, and social studies. These tangible, valuable benefits make incorporating a steel band into a school setting highly attractive.

HOW TO USE THIS BOOK

The chapters in this book are organized sequentially; the information is presented in an order that is conducive to initiating a program from the ground up. The components of the ensemble—instruments, personnel, and repertoire—are discussed first, followed by chapters on techniques and rehearsal strategies. However, readers should feel free to visit topics that apply to their own individual circumstances as they see fit. For instance, a person inheriting a program may already have instruments, and may therefore want to skip ahead to other topics.

At the end of the text you will find appendices that contain valuable resource information. A successful steel band director must continuously expand his or her knowledge through pertinent readings, collecting and listening to recordings, attending conferences and workshops, and interacting with others in the idiom. So, enjoy this book, but keep in mind that it is only a primer. When you have finished reading it, you will have taken the first step in a long journey, which, like all journeys in education, never truly ends.

ACKNOWLEDGMENTS

Writing a book is a difficult, painstaking process, especially for a first-time author. So my first thanks belong to my editors at MENC, Frances Ponick and Ashley Opp, for leading me through the development and refinement of my manuscript. I am particularly grateful to Fran who, despite my status as an unknown, believed both in me and in this project, and gave me a chance to create this resource. If it weren't for her, you would not be reading this book.

I have learned practically everything I know about pan by observing and interacting with a number of extremely talented pan artists over the years: Mat Britain, Darren Dyke, Gary Gibson, Robert Greenidge, Phil Hawkins, Ray Holman, Alan Lightner, Tom Miller, Jim Munzenrider, Andy Narell, Jeff Narell, Ken Philmore, Liam Teague. These artists, gifted as performers, teachers, and composers, are in a sense the true authors of this text. Among this fine group of musicians, I must especially recognize Tom Miller, who has become a great mentor and friend to both me and to my program at Miami University. I would also like to thank Ellie Mannette, whom I first met during my undergraduate years at West Virginia University. Ellie exemplifies perseverance, excellence, and attention to detail, and also the importance of sharing one's time and talents with others.

I must also thank my students at Miami University, who serve (knowingly or unknowingly!) as the sounding board and laboratory for all of my ideas. My students are my partners in music making; they are a continual source of inspiration and joy. I have also enjoyed terrific support from my colleagues in the Department of Music, and from my various administrators. I am blessed to have such a wonderful position at Miami.

Two of my former students (now colleagues in pan), Ed LeBorgne and Mike Marston, deserve mention. Both are high school steel band directors in southwest Ohio, and both read an early draft of the manuscript and offered insightful feedback.

Most importantly, my family is a great source of strength for me. Thanks to my parents, George and Ginny Tanner, for always encouraging me. Finally, a special thanks belongs to my wife, Donna. She is mother to my three beautiful sons, my biggest fan, and my rock of support.

❶

WHAT IS PAN?

The term *pan* is all encompassing. It not only is the preferred term for the instruments themselves (the term *steel drum* is misleading because pans are not in fact drums), but it also represents the art form in its entirety—the instruments, the people who build them, the bands, the performing artists, the composers and arrangers, and the music. This opening chapter offers some answers to the question, "What is pan?" Armed with a brief knowledge of our instrument's history, its common repertoire, and its passionate effect on those who play it, you'll hopefully become even more excited to jump into your own pan program.

PAN IS HISTORY

Trinidad is the birthplace of pan. Throughout the colonial period, a number of European powers held control of the island, eventually culminating in British rule in 1797. However, the French contributed perhaps one of the most significant cultural traditions—a tradition that eventually lead to the development of pan: the

Masquerade. A season of grand celebration held annually between Christmas and Lent, the Masquerade eventually became
known as Carnival. Similarly named periods of fêtes occur nowa-
days throughout the Caribbean.

Originally these festivities were the sole dominion of the elite,
ruling classes, but as time passed the lower classes of Trinidad society, including emancipated slaves, developed their own celebrations and traditions. Naturally, music was a part of Carnival, and
the lower-class participants relied on instruments that were readily
available to them, such as drums, and other simple percussion instruments. Often, percussion instruments were made from found
objects, such as an empty bottle struck with a spoon.

A detailed discussion of the sociopolitical history of Trinidad is
not warranted here; it suffices to say that the relationship between
the upper and lower classes at times was strained. Perhaps at Carnival time the differences between these two groups were the most
evident, as each group's celebrations were reflective of their place
in society. The lower class Mas' (short for Masquerade) became increasingly raucous as time passed, and the upper-class response
became more and more restrictive. Clashes between the poor and
the authorities led to riots during the 1881 Carnival, and then to a
law banning noisy musical instruments (the Peace Preservation
Ordinance) in 1884. With the passage of this law, drumming in the
streets was effectively quashed.

Tamboo Bamboo

Faced with the idea of having their musical expression silenced,
the lower classes explored other resources for creating the rhythmic accompaniments to their Carnival celebrations. In the 1890s,
people began cutting bamboo into various lengths, and either
stamping them on the ground or striking them against one another.
The rhythmic music made by these bamboo instruments trans-

ferred directly from commonly used drumming rhythms. In effect, the people drummed, but used bamboo instead of drums. Hence, these bamboo ensembles became collectively known as *tamboo bamboo*; the word *tamboo* comes from the French word for drum, *tambour*.

Bamboo, while plentiful on the island, is not a very sturdy material, especially when it is being banged on the ground for hours at a time during a Carnival parade. As a result, people became less and less enamored of tamboo bamboo as the twentieth century arrived. By the 1910s, tamboo bamboo bands had increasingly incorporated other sounds. Remember that found objects had played a part in the musical tradition of Trinidad for years. In addition to the likes of the bottle and spoon, bands began to experiment with metal containers of various sizes.

Metal Pan Bands

By the 1930s, metal containers had completely replaced bamboo as the primary source for rhythmic music. As in tamboo bamboo, the players in these metal pan bands were simply re-creating the rhythmic patterns that had been in use for generations. In other words, these instruments were exclusively rhythmic—the players were not yet tuning the containers purposefully, with the goal of creating resonant pitches.

However, some of the players did discover, somewhat accidentally, that the dented surface of a metal can could produce a definite pitch. The exact moment of such discovery is unknown, and we cannot precisely identify the first individuals who noticed this wonderful capability of dented metal. We do know that by the early 1940s, some players were creating pitched instruments on purpose. Discarded biscuit tins that were easily obtained from trash heaps, and industrial containers such as caustic soda barrels were two of the most commonly used types of metal can. These early, crude instruments typically comprised only a few roughly tuned pitches.

Important Innovations

Significant innovations in the 1940s and 1950s propelled these makeshift instruments onto a national, and then an international stage. For example, today pans appear as bowls, with the playing surface sunk into a concave shape. However, many early pans were created in the opposite fashion, with the playing surface rising up (as if the bowl were upside-down). The sinking of pans, such that the playing surface was concave, was one of the most important early innovations.

The use of wrapped sticks was another important development. Sticks had always been used to play the metal cans, but it was not until the 1940s that players began wrapping their sticks with some kind of soft material to minimize the contact sound. These days, pan sticks typically have rubber tubing on the beating end; in the 1940s, leaves were used!

Using large-diameter barrels as the raw material for pans was a highly significant innovation. The biscuit tins and caustic soda barrels of the 1930s had small diameters, and thus only a handful of pitch areas were possible. In the 1940s, some pan men began using discarded 55-gallon drums as the raw material for their instruments. The rest, as they say, is history. Today, the 55-gallon barrel remains an industry standard for those who craft pans, although some pan builders have begun moving away from the 55-gallon barrel in favor of crafting their own "barrels" from scratch.

Yet another improvement involves the use of straps or stands to suspend the instruments. At first, pan players used only one stick to strike the instrument, because their other hand held the instrument. In the 1940s, players began attaching straps to the barrels. The pans were suspended around the players' necks, and this style of playing (still practiced in a limited fashion) was known as *pan 'round de neck*. Pan 'round de neck allowed the players to use both hands as well as to be mobile, which meant that the instruments could be easily played in Carnival parades. Stands soon followed, allowing the players to play in a stationary position; this is currently the most common way of playing pan.

Initially, pans did not have a fully chromatic range of pitches; that is, many early pans did not contain all twelve pitches that we recognize in Western music. This lack of pitches meant that players could only perform tunes that used the particular set of pitches their pan contained. As Trinidadian musicians adapted diverse musical arrangements to the instruments, the pan builders soon realized the need to incorporate all twelve pitches onto each instrument, thereby eliminating this disadvantage.

Finally, the expansion of instrument types was essential for making ensemble music. The first pans created were melodic instruments. Soon, pan players realized the need for accompanying voices. In the 1940s and 1950s, chording voices and bass voices were added to the melodic pans, and the steel band was born. Various individuals over the years have been responsible for devising different types of pan, and thus no single person is responsible for creating the steel band as we know it today.

An Amazing Achievement

It is important to remember that pan players and creators in Trinidad were not professional inventors, scientists, or college professors. They were, by and large, poor young men from some of the roughest neighborhoods of Trinidad's large cities, such as Port-of-Spain and San Fernando. As such, the fact that they have been able to provide a gift to the world in the form of these wonderful instruments is nothing short of amazing. Trinidadians are fiercely proud of the steel pan; in fact, it has been declared the National Musical Instrument of Trinidad and Tobago.

The passion felt for these instruments is still strong today, and those entering the pan realm for the first time may find that its denizens often hold strong opinions regarding the instruments. Such loyalties are not hard to understand when you realize that some of the most seminal figures in the art form—builders, tuners, players, composers—are still alive today. Pan is a relatively young instrument, and its history is still being written.

PAN IS MUSIC

Pan is a wonderfully versatile instrument, capable of performing almost any style of music effectively. As a solo instrument, the steel pan is equally at home in the nightclub and the concert hall: pan artists such as Robert Greenidge and Ken "Professor" Philmore dazzle audiences with their virtuosic displays, Andy Narell and Othello Molineaux lead successful careers as jazz frontmen, while Liam Teague has performed concertos for pan and orchestra in prestigious art music venues. In an ensemble setting, not only is a diversity of styles interesting to both performers and audiences alike, but it is also, as we shall see in chapter 6, pedagogically sound. In short, the ability of pan to comfortably negotiate diverse musical environments and styles serves as a tremendous asset.

Of course, there is no doubt that its deep association with the music of the Caribbean, and in particular to the predominant Trinidadian musical styles, calypso and soca, draws a lot of folks to pan. These two styles are staples of the steel band repertoire; they are (and should be) conspicuously unavoidable to anyone who plays the instrument. The feel of calypso and soca is different than Western popular music. It has a rhythmic character, a lilt if you will, that words cannot describe, and it is difficult to hear it without being captivated by its intoxicating motion. Pan and calypso are inextricably linked, and likely will be so forever. And no pan player I know would have it any other way.

PAN IS PEOPLE

When you enter the world of pan, you encounter many colorful figures. The various individuals and groups who have touched the art form over the years create a marvelous mélange. First and foremost are the builders and tuners. Pan wouldn't exist without Ellie Mannette, Winston "Spree" Simon, Bertie Marshall, Anthony Williams, and Neville Jules, all of whom are widely recognized in the realm of pan as being chief innovators in the early days. These respected individuals were there when it all began, and are responsible for many of the developments discussed earlier in the chapter.

In addition to the builders and tuners, composers and arrangers have created, and continue to generate, outstanding music for steel band. For example, anyone playing in a steel band today should know the music of Len "Boogsie" Sharpe, Ray Holman, Andy Narell, and Tom Miller. There are others; these are a few notables. Each of these talented composers is also a superb performer. Another important group of artists to whom pan is eternally indebted are the calypsonians who have provided the source material for countless arrangements, such as The Mighty Sparrow, Lord Kitchener, and David Rudder, to name a few.

The people in your own steel band, however, are the most significant group of people in the pan world. You will find that a steel band creates a sense of community. Those in your band will form a bond because they will learn the instrument together as a group, not as individuals. They will make friendships and work together toward a common goal. Most importantly, they will share in the highly rewarding experience of bringing joy to audiences through the performance of popular music.

Furthermore, pan players experience camaraderie with other pan players around the world. One thing is for sure: pan people are passionate about what they do. This is not to say that other musicians are not equally passionate—but there is a palpable difference with pan. Most people who play pan feel as if they have discovered something special, something magical that most people still haven't heard about. For this reason, pan players tend to love what they do intensely, and they thoroughly enjoy sharing that love with others in their chosen sphere, in the same way that fans of a particular sports squad—despite being complete strangers—will behave as lifelong friends when their team gets the big win.

Trinidadians have a saying: "Pan is we ting." They are proud to claim ownership of pan, and we should be equally proud to represent this instrument and the Trinidadian culture from whence it hails. Like any artistic endeavor, pan will change over time. Yet anyone who becomes part of this body should make it a point to connect themselves, their band members, and their audiences with the roots of pan. You can achieve this in a number of ways: program some calypso or soca music; incorporate a demonstration of tamboo bamboo into your concert; include historical notes in your printed programs. The bottom line is to always keep the humble yet profound origins of this fantastic instrument in mind. Pan is an extraordinary gift, and we get to share that gift with others—what a delight!

②

PURCHASING INSTRUMENTS FOR YOUR STEEL BAND

As with any instrument, personal taste can enter into the selection process. Nonetheless, prospective buyers should be aware of certain fundamental qualities of steel pan instruments, so that they are able to form qualitative judgments before making a purchase. Unfortunately, it is often not possible to evaluate instruments firsthand. Pans are not widely popular, nor are they mass produced, and as a result you cannot find them on display at the local music store. In fact, pan builders are few and far between, and thus the simple reality of geography may make it impractical for one to visit a builder's workshop. If, as is typical, a director cannot inspect prospective purchases, then he or she should seek reputable references who can testify to the quality of the instruments. Buyers should not be hesitant to request builders to provide such references.

Most pan manufacturers do not keep instruments in stock; instead, the manufacturer begins crafting an instrument only after an order has been placed. To begin work, some builders require a down payment. It is common among pan builders for backlogs of orders to develop, so a significant period of wait time usually occurs between placing an order and actual delivery of the instruments.

This wait period can vary from one manufacturer to the next: a typical delay takes four to six months, but some buyers have had to wait over a year to receive their instruments. Anyone wishing to purchase pans should make an inquiry regarding the expected wait time with each prospective builder or firm they contact.

FAQ: Must I buy all of the instruments for my ensemble from the same builder?

Often when making an initial start-up purchase of instruments, a director acquires them from a single source. Then, when the director wants to later add instruments to the ensemble, he or she will purchase the additional pans from the same source, thereby maintaining consistency in terms of quality and timbre. However, buying all of one's pans from a single source is not necessarily essential, at least from a tone production standpoint. Many steel bands exist with instruments made by several different builders, and they can achieve a blended ensemble sound.

THE COST OF PANS

Anyone undertaking even a brief survey of pan costs will find a broad range of prices. A lead pan, for example can range in cost from $700 to $5,000. Prospective buyers are often confused as to why the variation in price is so great from one builder to the next. In truth, there are numerous reasons why the cost of pans varies so much. The first factor is simply one of economics. When comparing Trinidadian-made instruments to those crafted in the States, for instance, one may find that Trinidadian-made instruments are often less expensive. This is due in part to the differences between the Trinidadian and U.S. economies. In Trinidad, the weaker economy means that the builder's costs (materials, labor) are generally less than those of the U.S. builder.

Secondly, because pans are hand crafted, builders subjectively determine their price. A builder must ask the rhetorical question, "What is my time and expertise worth?" It is easy to understand that every builder is not going to have the same answer to this question. Of course, the market influences the value of any product. Many pan builders today still operate as individuals (as opposed to corporations), so the personal value judgments that builders make regarding the investment of time and energy they put into crafting instruments weigh heavily in the cost determination process.

A third explanation for the disparity in pan prices is that pan builders are crafting instruments for a wide variety of clients: professionals, amateurs, beginners, schools, community groups, and so on. The needs of these diverse individuals or groups are not the same. An analogy: a middle school is probably not going to spend $60,000 on a Steinway baby grand piano for their music classroom, but a university music department might see such a purchase as essential. In short, not every pan builder necessarily caters to the same clientele.

There may always be disparity in the cost of pans. The main point that prospective buyers need to understand is that cost does *not necessarily* indicate quality. For example, a $2,000 lead pan from builder A is not necessarily twice as good as a $1,000 lead pan from builder B. Pan as an art form is still young enough that market forces have not yet evened the playing field. Remember, many pan builders still operate as individuals, and may have established a comfortable clientele through word-of-mouth advertising only. Such a builder is not under the same kind of market pressure as a corporation. As time goes by and more people buy pans, the market will likely begin to dictate certain price "tiers," as has happened with wind and string instruments. Until that time, prospective buyers should evaluate instruments based on their inherent qualities, not on relative price.

WHAT MAKES A GOOD PAN?

We have seen that pans do not have the same timbre from one builder to the next, and we have learned that instruments' costs are widely variable and cannot necessarily serve as an indicator of quality. So, how exactly does one comparatively assess these instruments? The answer lies in comparing the physical characteristics, workmanship, and tone. A quality instrument has the following characteristics:

Condition of the Steel
> A well-crafted pan is free of dents or blemishes on either the face or the skirt.

Finish
> Today, only two acceptable finishes are applied to pans, and many manufacturers offer both. The first type is sometimes referred to as an "auto body"–style finish. This finish involves a base coat–clear coat paint process similar to that employed on automobiles: the skirt and face of the pan are covered first with a thin layer of colored paint, followed by a clear protective coat. The other type of finish acceptable for pans is chrome plate. Both finishes are easy to maintain, and so the decision to choose one over the other may simply be one of personal taste. However, a chrome finish is generally viewed as superior to a paint finish, and thus when a builder offers both types of finish, chromed pans almost always cost more than painted ones.

Workmanship
> One can assess the amount of time and care put into creating a pan by looking for hammer blows on the face. Hammer blows appear as tiny crescents or half-moons, and indicate that the maker did not take the time to smooth them out through a process called *peening*. Peening involves using a small hammer with a very flat surface to strike the face of the pan many times,

removing all traces of hammer marks. A well-crafted pan has a face that looks as smooth as glass, especially in the dead spaces surrounding the pitch areas.

Consistency of Sound

Every pitch area of the pan should resonate comparably; a high-quality pan is consistent with regard to sound decay time, sensitivity (i.e., each pitch area within a given register produces tone with similar effort), and tuning. If only one register of the pan sounds good (for example, high pitches sound acceptable but low pitches sound muddy or undefined), then the pan may be of lesser quality.

Remember, because buyers commonly do not see the instruments that they purchase in advance, they should inspect them closely upon delivery. If a buyer feels that the product is defective in any way, he or she should not feel uncomfortable returning it for either a refund or a replacement.

ARE 55-GALLON BARRELS OBSOLETE?

In the past few years, a few pan builders have begun crafting pans from scratch, abandoning the 55-gallon barrel as a starting point for creating the instruments. This behavior represents a break from over fifty years of tradition, as pan makers have been using 55-gallon barrels as the source material for pans since the mid-1940s.

The primary advantage for pan builders in crafting their own "barrels" from scratch is that the diameter is no longer restricted to that of the standard 55-gallon barrel, measuring just 22.5 inches across. Thus, a pan builder using this method can create pans with larger diameters, enabling them to increase the size of the pitch areas and to separate each pitch area from one another (as opposed to having pitch areas that share a common border). Builders who employ this new method of pan crafting claim that they can achieve a superior tone quality, resonance, and tuning in doing so. Having personally compared these large-diameter pans with their 55-gallon counterparts, I find it hard to dispute these claims.

However, prospective buyers will find that pans crafted in this way cost more—sometimes significantly so—than pans made from 55-gallon barrels. As a result, directors faced with the hard realities of tight budgets may not be able to purchase instruments of this type. What's more, at this writing only a small minority of builders is offering this "new generation" of pan. So, it appears that the 55-gallon barrel is still with us, at least for a little while longer.

THE ROLE OF PAN TUNING

Anyone purchasing steel pans must be aware at the outset of the role that tuning plays in the life of these instruments. With respect to tuning, a pan is like a piano in several ways:

- Tuning is one of the final steps in the process of crafting the instrument.
- The instrument goes out of tune through regular (albeit sometimes vigorous!) use.
- Only a skilled professional can tune the instrument.
- Tuning the instrument is a regular process that must be performed periodically throughout the life of the instrument.

In an ensemble setting, it is recommended that pans be tuned once each year. Thus, anyone starting a steel band must understand that tuning is a continuous expense that must be budgeted for annually. Those who neglect this aspect of pan ownership are doing a disservice to themselves, their members, and pan in general (not to mention their audiences).

WHAT EXACTLY MAKES PANS GO OUT OF TUNE?

Pans are tuned by shaping the various pitch areas using different sizes of hammers: each individually sized area on the face, shaped a certain way, resonates at a certain pitch. Pans must be handled and played with care, so as to avoid knocking the various pitch areas out of shape, and thus out of tune. These concepts are especially important to ingrain in band members, as in most cases they themselves do not personally own the instruments, and they may be apt to handle them with less care than if they owned the instrument themselves. If a pan is dropped, or bumped going through a doorway, for example, the tuning can be affected.

Playing the pan with too much force can knock pitches out of tune. For this reason, beginners must be instructed early on as to the proper technique for striking the instruments. Directors should keep in mind that once a pitch on a pan is out of tune, it will remain that way until a tuner fixes it; in other words, one may have to live with that out-of-tune pitch for quite a while.

THE TUNER

Tuners (often this term is used to designate persons who both build *and* tune steel pans) are usually most comfortable working on instruments that they have built, but many tuners are also at ease tuning instruments not of their own construction. Preferably, the builder of the instruments also tunes them whenever possible, because the builder intimately knows his or her own product.

Sometimes, a tuner who works on instruments made by another tuner attempts to change the timbre of the instruments to match his or her own personal sound concept. When this occurs, it sometimes "confuses" the instruments, and they may no longer resonate as they were originally intended. Owners should be able to describe the sound they want to hear from their instruments, in layman's terms (such as bright, dark, strident, mellow), so that a tuner understands what kind of timbre the owner desires. In any case, your best bet is to purchase instruments that inherently have the sound you want, and then to instruct any tuner who works with the instruments to simply maintain that timbre.

Tuners are few, so having one's pans tuned is often not an easy task to accomplish. Pan players or directors ultimately face two options: either the instruments must be shipped or otherwise transported to the tuner's workshop, or the tuner must visit personally to do an on-site tuning. In either case, you will incur additional expenses aside from the actual tuning fee. Tuners have different methods of determining a tuning fee. Some tuners charge by the hour, while others charge by the piece. On average, one should expect to pay between $100 and $175 per instrument for tuning fees. Again, it cannot be emphasized too strongly that tuning is an essential facet of having a steel band program, and that directors must plan in advance for this annual expense.

One final comment here: pan tuning has evolved in the past several decades to a point that the process is highly sophisticated. Only an expert craftsperson with years of experience can tune a pan effectively. Thus, directors or players with no experience in tuning should *never* attempt to take a hammer to their instruments. To do so is to invite disaster. Only a qualified individual or firm should be allowed to tune the instruments.

SUPPORTING EQUIPMENT FOR PANS

Three areas of supporting equipment directly concern pans: mallets, stands, and cases. Rhythm section instruments such as drumset and conga drums may also be considered to be supporting equipment, but these and other rhythm section items and issues will be addressed in detail in chapter 8, "The Engine Room."

Mallets

These days steel pan mallets are constructed of either wooden or hollow aluminum shafts, with rubber tubing placed on the beating end of the mallet. Mallets differ for each instrument type: those for upper-register instruments (lead, double tenor, double second) require less mass on the beating end, and the shafts are usually around eight to nine inches in length. Mallets for guitar and cello pans have more layers of rubber on the end, and feature longer shafts (approximately ten inches). Bass pan mallets typically have a shaped rubber ball on the end instead of rubber tubing.

It is important to use the correct type of mallet for each instrument type, since using an incorrect mallet can affect the tone of the instrument adversely. Pan manufacturing companies typically offer pan mallets for purchase, with a cost range of between $15 and $30 for each pair, depending on the manufacturer and the type of mallet.

There are two strategies for mallet ownership in steel band programs. One strategy requires all members to purchase and own their own mallets. While this practice can instill a sense of personal responsibility, it can be a financial burden for members who may play more than one instrument. In this case, the second strategy, in which all mallets in the ensemble are community property and owned by the band, may prove more viable. Of course, directors who employ this strategy may find that certain members still want to own their own mallets.

Regardless of what you decide to do concerning mallets, you should purchase a spare set—at least one pair for each instrument type—to have for emergencies. This emergency set should be taken on every off-campus performance, in case someone in the band forgets his or her mallets.

Stands

When a pan is purchased, a stand should come with it, except in the case of bass pans, which are often free-standing instruments with feet attached to the bottoms of the barrels. Sometimes, a pan builder includes an introductory-level stand made simply from electrical conduit. Conduit stands work fine, are light, and break down into three component parts easily (two legs and a cross beam). The disadvantages of conduit stands are that they are cumbersome—the legs are usually at least 3.5 feet high and do not collapse—and they are not adjustable. Most alternatives to the conduit stand offered by pan manufacturers are height-adjustable, allowing the player to easily raise or lower the instrument.

In evaluating stands for purchase, the director may want to consider the following factors:

Cost
> Some manufacturers offer several types of pan stand, with a range of prices.

Durability
> If the ensemble does much traveling and gigging, then durability is a concern. A gigging band needs stands that hold up to the wear and tear of the road. Another related factor involves how the stands break down: a band that travels often may want to find stands that break down and go back together with ease.

Weight and Bulk
> Possibly another important factor for gigging bands, lighter, less cumbersome stands may be more desirable than heavy ones if your members are going to have to cart them to and fro numerous times.

Wheels
> Some manufacturers offer stands with castors, or the option of castors applied to certain stand models. Having castors on stands allows for ease of mobility that can allow players to adjust the position of the stands quickly. Some pan stands that feature castors also feature wheel locks, so that the stands can be fixed in one place during performance.

Cases

Cases for each pan are important to have for both storage and transport purposes. Though obvious, pans constitute a significant financial investment, so protecting them is imperative. As with stands, many pan manufacturers offer cases as part of their product lines, but you can also purchase them through music stores and catalogs.

Both soft and hard cases are available for pans. Soft cases do not offer as much protection, but they take up less space. Hard cases are made from some type of plastic (different case manufacturers use different types of material), and can better protect your investment. Some companies offer cases with castors for bass pans and other long-skirted instruments. While castors on such cases increase the cost, they make moving the instruments much easier.

Also now available on the market are cases (usually designed for upper-voice pans like lead or double second) with suitcase-style handles and wheels. These suitcase-style cases are wonderful for the soloist who must schlep his instruments around by himself, but directors should know that the attached handles on these cases do not allow them to be stacked on top of one another easily. This can be a negative for large ensembles: stacking cases is important not only to maximize one's storage space, but also to load cases into a truck, say, for transportation to a gig.

Carefully choosing, maintaining, and protecting your instruments and supporting equipment will start your pan program off right.

3

THE FIVE MOST COMMON INSTRUMENT TYPES

This chapter introduces the five most common instrument types found in the steel band today. Regardless of type, all pans have three standard components: a *face*, which is the convex, bowl-shaped surface where the beating spots are located; a *skirt*, which consists of the side walls of the barrel and varies in length depending on the instrument type; and a *rim*, which connects the face to the skirt. Pans are either suspended on stands, or they may be freestanding, depending on the length of the skirt. Instruments with long skirts that extend nearly to the floor are often freestanding.

The lack of standardization among pans is manifest in several ways, the most significant of which involves the *pitch layout*, or the arrangement of pitch areas on the face. Simply put, if one were to examine an instrument type from one builder and compare the pitch layout to that of the same instrument type made by a different builder, one may find variances. In some cases, these variances are not subtle. While this lack of standardization may not pose a problem to individual players, a director must be aware of this idiosyncrasy. You do not want to purchase instruments of the same type from different builders without first verifying that the pitch layouts are identical.

Keep in mind that pans are by and large handcrafted instruments. As such, each pan maker can create a unique product. This does not mean that there is significant inconsistency from one pan to the next in a particular builder's output; on the contrary, the art of crafting pans has arrived, after years of discovery, experimentation, and refinement, to the place where an accomplished builder can create quality instruments consistently. Rather, the point is that from builder to builder, pans may *sound* different: each individual builder or firm has their own way of approaching the crafting process, and these differences often lead to variations (sometimes pronounced) in timbre. Thus, it is possible to have instruments of comparable quality and workmanship that nonetheless sound different from one another.

The following lists the five most common instrument types in the steel band, in score order, proceeding from highest to lowest register. All pans read at concert pitch.

FAQ: What is a bore pan?

Some manufacturers offer bore pans in their product lines. A bore pan features tiny holes drilled through the face of the instrument, along the borders of each pitch area. Builders that offer bore pans as part of their product lines often claim that these instruments have either increased resonance or a more strident tone. Bore pans are certainly not as common as "normal" (non-bore) ones, and their generally bright timbre represents just one of the many different timbres found in the diverse realm of pan. Whether or not to purchase bore pans comes down, in the end, to a matter of personal taste.

Figure 3.1   Lead pan approximate range

LEAD PAN

The instrument known as a *lead pan* (*lead* rhymes with *need*) is the only type of pan that comprises one barrel. Every other type of pan comprises multiple barrels, from two to as many as twelve. The lead pan has the highest register of all instruments in the steel band, and its function in the band is almost exclusively melodic.

Terminology for this instrument is somewhat muddled. A lead pan can also be known as a *tenor pan* or a *soprano pan*. Both instrument builders and music arrangers may employ any one of these three designations. Steel band directors must understand that all three of these names refer to the same instrument type.

Lead pans may have several different pitch layouts, but the most common layout is often called a "circle of fifths pan," because the pitches are arranged in an inverted circle of fifths. With a "C-lead," the lowest pitch available is middle C. Many lead pans have the D above middle C as the lowest pitch; these are often called "D-leads." The range of the lead pan is typically between two and one third to two and one half octaves, as shown in figure 3.1.

DOUBLE TENOR PAN

The *double tenor pan* is usually orchestrated as a melodic instrument, often doubling the lead pan line in unison or an octave below, or harmonizing the lead pan line in homorhythmic fashion. It is distinguished from the other double drum type, the double second pan,

**Figure 3.2   Double tenor pan approxi-
mate range**

primarily by its pitch layout; the register and range (approximately
two and one half octaves) of the two instruments is nearly identical.

DOUBLE SECOND PAN

The *double second pan* comprises two barrels, and upon casual ob-
servation can appear very much like the double tenor. The primary
difference between the double tenor pan and the double second
pan is in the pitch layout. While the layout of the double second is
not standardized from one builder to the next, a distinguishing feature of the double second is the use of whole tone scales. Each barrel of a double second pan contains the pitches of a whole tone
scale: the right barrel contains the whole tone scale that begins
with F, while the left barrel contains the whole tone scale that begins with E. The double second pan, like the double tenor pan, can
be used as a melodic instrument in a band setting, but the instrument most often provides harmonic support.

**Figure 3.3   Double second pan approx-
imate range**

GUITAR PAN/CELLO PAN

The names *guitar pan* and *cello pan* represent one of the most con-
fusing elements of the steel band idiom with regard to terminology.

Figure 3.4 Triple guitar/triple cello pan approximate range

The terms "guitar" and "cello" can not only be found in the catalogs of instrument makers, but also on sheet music arrangements (where the hybrid term "guitar/cello" is also prevalent). Some instrument makers only build guitars; some only build cellos. Some arrangements have guitar parts; some have cello parts. Still other arrangements have both a guitar *and* a cello part.

To make sense of this confusion, let us approach these instruments as a class or category. First, the class of instruments known as either guitar pans or cello pans typically occupies a register that is below that of the double-set instruments. The skirt length of these instruments can vary, from around seventeen inches to more than twenty-seven inches. Guitar pans and cello pans can comprise two, three, or four barrels: the most common instrument names are double guitar, triple guitar, triple cello, four-cello.

The range and register (figure 3.4) of all of the instruments in this class are similar, regardless of the number of barrels used to create the instrument. This instrument type in a band setting typically provides harmonic support, although guitar pans/cello pans sometimes perform countermelodies or double the bass line. Steel band directors who encounter instruments named *guitar* or *cello* should view such instruments as essentially the same in terms of their function.

BASS PAN

The *bass pan* has the lowest register in the ensemble and underpins the music both harmonically and rhythmically. Typically, bass pans comprise six barrels, although some manufacturers craft bass

Figure 3.5   Bass pan approximate range

pans consisting of eight, nine, or twelve barrels. However, a set of bass pans with six barrels provides a sufficient range. Bass pans feature a full skirt length, representing the entire length of a 55-gallon barrel.

Some makers offer an instrument called a *tenor bass* (or *tenor-bass*), comprising only four barrels. This instrument not only has a smaller range than the bass pan, but its register is also approximately a half octave higher. As a result, the tenor bass alone does not provide enough "punch" in the lower register to support a full ensemble by itself. The tenor bass can, however, serve as a complement to the bass pan, provided that the ensemble has a sufficient representation of bass pans already. Bottom line: the tenor bass should not be seen as a substitute for the bass pan.

4

DEVELOPING YOUR STEEL BAND'S INSTRUMENTATION

Armed with a basic knowledge of the common instrument types found in a steel band, a prospective steel band director still faces an important challenge: selecting a specific instrumentation for his or her ensemble. Of course, financial constraints often play a considerable role in such decisions. Nevertheless, a new director (or one that desires to grow his or her program) must tackle the question of exactly what instrument types to purchase.

THE ROLE OF REPERTOIRE

Repertoire can decidedly influence the selection or development of the instrumentation for your steel band, because the genres and sources of repertoire that a director chooses to pursue bear directly upon the instrumentation necessary to realize it. A detailed discussion of repertoire for the steel band takes place in chapter 6, but I must address the issue here briefly because it directly impacts purchasing choices that take place at the genesis of a program.

Over the past twenty years, a number of publishing houses devoted either fully or partially to steel band literature have arisen, compelling composers and arrangers to dedicate their work to print. In that time, a relatively standard orchestration has evolved that incorporates five distinct parts: two melodic parts (often lead and double tenor), two harmonic parts (often double second and guitar/cello), and a bass part.

While this five-voice orchestration is not universal, it is prevalent, particularly in compositions or arrangements that fall into the various popular music styles so common in the steel band repertoire—not only Trinidadian popular styles such as calypso and soca, but also other Latin, Caribbean, and American popular styles of music. Thus, if a director intends to perform published arrangements and compositions frequently, then he or she should adopt an instrumentation that can cover five distinct parts.

On the other hand, if a director intends to provide repertoire for the ensemble through his or her own arranging (a practice that is certainly valid and can in fact be preferable, particularly if the director works with members who for whatever reason cannot realize written notation), then the ensemble's instrumentation need not conform to this five-voice orchestration model. In such cases, a four-voice orchestration (such as lead, double second, guitar/cello, bass) suffices and can effectively realize arrangements in the melody and accompaniment texture common to most popular music.

CREATING SECTIONS

Another important consideration when developing the instrumentation for a steel band involves the idea of creating sections of instrument types. Several reasons show why it is good practice to have more than one instrument of each representative type in one's ensemble.

First, having sections of each instrument type in the ensemble allows for increased volume. In this way, sections in the steel band mimic the same practice of, say, the string sections of symphony orchestras or the various woodwind or brass sections of a wind band. Second, it is simply practical to have more than one instrument of every type so that players are not solely responsible for that musical part. In such a "chamber music"–style scenario, the margin for error among the players decreases dramatically—let alone the nightmare scenario of having one (or more) members out sick on the night of a performance. Third, having an increased number of instruments in the ensemble means simply that more members can participate in the ensemble.

Finally, directors must understand that some advanced literature for steel band calls for expanded orchestrations, with six or even seven distinct parts. In such cases, composers typically create additional harmony parts that expand the orchestration; these added lines are commonly scored for either double second pan or guitar/cello pan. Thus, if the director intends to approach advanced literature of this type, having multiple instruments of these mid-range instrument types (double second, guitar/cello) is essential.

DOUBLE TENOR OR DOUBLE SECOND?

As mentioned in chapter 3, the double tenor pan and the double second pan differ from one another primarily in terms of their pitch layout. There is no real difference in register or range, any difference in timbre can be considered negligible (especially in a large band setting), and a player only exposed to one of the types will not be concerned with the idiomatic challenges or technical demands of the other. Thus, a director may rightly ask: is having both of these instrument types in a band absolutely necessary?

The short answer is no. Either one of these double-set instruments could serve a band well, although one can make an argument for choosing the double second pan simply because today it has far wider use than the double tenor pan. Because the former is far more common than the latter, double second players who move from one band to another are more likely to encounter their instruments in their new ensemble than are double tenor players. Another consequence of the double second's popularity is that most builders offer it in their product lines, whereas many builders choose not to offer the double tenor.

Preferences aside, one thing is certain: directors must acquire enough double sets to adequately cover all of the parts provided in whatever repertoire the band pursues. To illustrate this point, consider the following example: a director has enough resources to initially purchase ten steel pan instruments, and he has decided to only purchase double second pans, forgoing the double tenor pan altogether. Two possible instrumentation scenarios that incorporate only four instrument types follow:

Scenario 1	*Scenario 2*
4 lead pans	2 lead pans
2 double second pans	4 double second pans
2 guitar pans	2 guitar pans
2 bass pans	2 bass pans

Scenario 1 would be excellent for realizing four-part orchestrations: the band would have a satisfactory balance with four melodic voices (the lead pans), four harmonic voices (the double second and guitar pans), and two bass voices. However, if the director wants to pursue any music with five-part orchestrations—the norm for published steel band literature—then scenario 1 would not work very well. In a five-part orchestration, there are almost always two double-set parts (usually a melodic double tenor part and a harmonic double second part).

In such a case, only one player under scenario 1 could cover each double-set part. Using one or two lead pan players to cover one of the double-set parts is not a viable option, because the double-set parts likely extend below the register of the lead pan. Thus scenario 2 is clearly the better instrumentation choice for realizing five-part orchestrations: the director could simply assign two of the double second players to play the double tenor part.

Having both the double tenor pan and the double second pan in the ensemble is certainly not necessary if the ensemble only performs music orchestrated for four parts. If the ensemble plays music orchestrated for five (or more) parts, then having both types, though not absolutely necessary, still remains an option. Consider scenario 2 above: if the director wanted to have both double-set instrument types, the breakdown of voices would be:

Scenario 2 (with five instrument types)
2 lead pans
2 double tenor pans
2 double second pans
2 guitar pans
2 bass pans

Guitar Pan versus Cello Pan

Keep in mind that in a practical sense, the difference between a guitar pan and a cello pan is mainly one of nomenclature. If a director purchases pans from a builder who offers both a guitar pan and a cello pan, then he or she probably does not need to purchase both types. Bottom line: a steel band essentially needs only one instrument type (not one *instrument*, mind you) from the guitar/cello classification, so practical considerations may influence the decision-making process when purchasing guitars or cellos. For instance, a director may ask herself: do I want three-barrel or four-barrel guitar/cello instruments? Three-barrel instruments mean one less barrel to carry on a gig, and one less case to buy. Of course, this kind of question should not be the sole basis for making instrument purchase decisions. All things being equal, practical questions may be worth asking, particularly in situations where financial resources are limited.

STRATEGIES FOR GROWTH

A steel band director often does not have the financial resources to purchase all of the instruments that she wants initially. As a result, the ensemble may not have an ideal instrumentation at the outset. Directors should have a plan for growing the ensemble over a period of time. By having an eventual, final instrumentation in mind, directors can make purchases, as finances allow, that gradually move toward realizing that goal. Some pan manufacturers offer package deals on instruments. While buying a package deal may be beneficial from a financial standpoint, directors should nonetheless ask the manufacturer if substitutions are possible. In this way, the director still might take advantage of a package discount, while simultaneously tailoring the instrumentation to fit his or her long-term goals.

Directors have two basic ways in which they can approach building their ensemble over time. They may initially purchase a set of instruments that contains at least one of every desired instrument type. In this plan, the director would simply proceed to create sections of instrument types by gradually adding instruments.

The second path involves purchasing an initial set of instruments without some of the desired types, with the understanding that she will add these types later. In either case, the director could employ the pans in several "unconventional" ways, while biding her time. For example, a director with a limited pan instrumentation could fold what pans she had into an existing jazz ensemble or traditional percussion ensemble, or she could treat the pans as an actual steel band while augmenting the pan parts with percussion keyboard instruments such as marimba or vibraphone.

There are no established standards regarding the optimal size of a steel band. The steel band director must tailor the size of the band to his or her own needs, resources, and mission for the ensemble. Directors must, however, consider balance when developing their band's instrumentation. Sections should not be underrepresented, especially the lead pan section. Because the lead pans almost always carry the melody, they must be heard. To achieve balance the lead pan section should generally have the greatest representation of all the sections in the ensemble.

ELECTRIC BASS VERSUS PAN BASS

Some steel band directors choose to use electric bass rather than bass pans to cover bass parts. This practice is completely acceptable, and quite pragmatic under certain circumstances. First, the director may already have access to an electric bass, thereby eliminating the cost of purchasing bass pans. With a tight budget, a director initiating a steel band could make a sacrifice in the bass area, possibly eliminating the need to sacrifice elsewhere in the band. For example, if faced with only enough funding to purchase initially only four instruments, eliminate the bass pan and use electric bass for a while.

Second, taking a bass guitar and an amplifier on a gig is much less cumbersome than hauling six full-size barrels. Third, if the director teaches in a school with a jazz ensemble, there is likely at least one student capable of playing the bass guitar who could easily enter the steel band.

While it is true that the electric bass can easily cover bass pan parts (albeit adjusting for register), and that some listeners actually favor the sound of the electric bass in a steel band, a steel band that does not have bass pans simply has something missing. The bass pans provide a percussive punch and a feeling in the gut that can simply not be replicated by any other instrument. Once a director—and the band members—have experienced the powerful presence of a bass pan section, they almost certainly will not want to give it up.

5

PERSONNEL

The overall mission of any steel band ensemble directly impacts the decisions involved in selecting personnel. Depending on the goals of the ensemble, the membership is either inclusive or exclusive. This chapter explains the relative merits of both, and provides strategies for assigning personnel to specific instrument types. It also addresses the advantages of having a tiered program that separates beginners from experienced players.

THE INCLUSIVE APPROACH

A steel band director may decide to create an inclusive ensemble in which all comers are welcome, regardless of musical ability, potential, or experience. A few examples of environments where such an approach may be appropriate include public schools with at-risk populations, community-based institutions, or churches. In these places, the reasons for creating a steel band extend beyond the realm of music making. In fact, some individuals may deem such considerations more important than music making! These reasons might be summed up as "community building"; in other words, the steel band serves primarily as an outlet for people to come together and participate in a communal activity. Playing music is a mere by-product of such interaction. Steel band lends itself quite well to this mission. First, it is easy for beginners, even for people with very limited musical talents, to enjoy early success making acceptable sounds on a pan. There are no embouchures to train, no bows to hold, no large batteries of keys to depress. One simply strikes the pan on a pitch area, and sound comes forth. Of course, playing pan requires more than merely making a sound emanate from the instrument. The fact remains, though, that starting a player on pan is much easier than, for example, starting a person on clarinet or viola.

Second, steel band has extraordinarily broad possibilities with regard to repertoire. A steel band can play everything from Bach to Belafonte, and an astute director can choose repertoire to suit his or her particular constituency. While the church group may be interested in adapting hymns or contemporary worship songs, the junior high middle school students may want to play the latest hip-hop hit. The great flexibility in repertoire means that a steel band can be a highly versatile ensemble.

Third, the steel band can expose people to a wonderfully rich, non-Western culture: that of Trinidad. In fact, because steel bands often play other Latin and Caribbean styles such as samba, reggae, and beguine in addition to Trinidadian calypso and soca, the steel band can serve as an opportunity for exploring diverse styles of music.

Finally, playing in a steel band is *fun*. In my opinion, a steel band generates more excitement and energy among its members than any other group. What better type of ensemble to incorporate into a curriculum if one wants to draw people into the music program? All in all, an inclusive steel band can be a very successful undertaking, while at the same time producing viable and entertaining music.

THE EXCLUSIVE APPROACH

Some directors favor an exclusive approach in determining personnel. In these situations, the director must determine the admission criteria for the ensemble. For example, a high school band director starting a steel band program may stipulate that all members of the steel band be already enrolled in either band or choir. This practice would parallel many high school jazz ensembles: the jazz ensemble is often seen as a complementary activity to traditional wind band or orchestra, instead of a substitute or replacement for it.

By and large, exclusive steel bands comprise personnel that come to the activity with prior musical training or experience; this often implies that the players can read music notation. By adopting such criteria, the director ensures a base level of musicianship among the members that in turn reduces the amount of rehearsal time the director must devote to teaching the fundamentals of music. Instead, the band can spend rehearsal time working on literature. Of course, a band that can read music does not necessarily always perform better than a band that cannot; rather, the difference is one of mission. In an educational setting, where reading music notation constitutes the standard for all other music ensembles, why should the steel band be any different?

Some institutions may have room for both inclusive and exclusive ensembles. For instance, a high school steel band director could have two separate steel band "tracks": one for the general student population that welcomes everyone to participate, and one for students already in the music program. Naturally, the goals and expectations for these two different groups would be inherently different because they serve different purposes. It must be emphasized that both approaches are valid and can be rewarding to their respective members.

One reason why a director might avoid the above situation is simply lack of time. Band, choir, or orchestra directors often develop a steel band program as an extracurricular activity. In these cases, the instruction represents an overload for the director. While the benefits of a steel band are numerous, and a director may also find the activity to be invigorating, teachers must cautiously avoid overload and burnout. Directors should consider developing a new steel band program gradually, so they don't suddenly create an unmanageable time commitment.

HOLDING AUDITIONS

Auditions may be necessary when a director needs to select appropriate personnel for the ensemble. One thing about steel band auditions that is different from the practice of most other ensemble auditions is that the steel band audition need not involve playing a steel pan at all. Remember that most people auditioning for a steel band, while they may have previous experience singing or playing a musical instrument, likely have never seen a steel pan up close. As a result, their complete unfamiliarity with the instrument may actually cloud the audition process.

Directors should thus consider making the audition for steel band purely a test of musical ability. The audition could primarily comprise pitch recognition (in either bass or treble clef, or both) and rhythmic sight-reading in various time signatures. These abilities can be tested without the use of *any* instrument. Of course, directors may incorporate some minimal pan playing into the audition, just to see how readily a person could adapt to the instrument. However, this element of the audition perhaps ought to be considered only minimally in the overall evaluation of a candidate.

Directors who use auditions might want to keep the following suggestions in mind. First, have more than one person hear the auditions. Listening to auditions can be tiring: it is difficult to remember what the second candidate sounded like when one is listening to the fourteenth candidate, for example. Having another set of ears in auditions can be invaluable when the time comes to tabulate data and make close decisions. If a director works alone, and no other music expert is on staff, then the director may consider asking a trusted musician from the community to sit in on the audition. Remember: it is not essential that your helper be a pan player, if you are simply testing for musical ability and potential. In many cases, there won't be another pan player or steel band for miles around.

Second, test for hand dexterity. Some instruments in the steel band, such as the lead pan, require a fair amount of hand dexterity. Members who come to the steel band experience from a percussion background would likely fare well as lead pan players, because they have experience in manipulating sticks or mallets. Conversely, non-percussionists may not be able, at least at the outset, to handle sticks with any degree of finesse. Having some

---

FAQ: What is strumming?

Strumming in the context of a steel band gets its name from the comparable behavior found in guitar playing. When a guitar player strums, he plays the tones of a chord using a rhythmic ostinato. When a pan player strums, he does the same thing, although he is limited to only playing two members of the chord at a time, because two mallets are generally all he is capable of holding.

Instruments in the mid-range of the ensemble, such as the double seconds and the triple guitars or cellos, are often the ones that have strumming parts in an arrangement (in fact the steel pan type known as the *guitar* is so named because its function in the band traditionally is to strum chords!). Players will often find strumming difficult, primarily because arrangers use syncopated rhythms to create the strum patterns. Also, a strummer is not playing melody, so the part can be hard to memorize (imagine playing only the left-hand part of a piano score).

method of determining to what degree a player can handle sticks is important not only in terms of admission to the band, but also in terms of what instrument type they may be suited for. Third, make an effort to identify potential strummers. Personnel who end up playing chording instruments in the band (for example, double second pan, guitar/cello pan) must be able to strum. In the auditions, if you can identify people that have the ability to play syncopated ostinatos consistently, then you have identified your strummers. Test for this ability by having candidates clap idiomatic strum rhythms while keeping a beat with their feet, for example.

Finally, designing a table for keeping track of audition data makes tabulating results at the end of the auditions much easier. You can draft an audition table to cater to your particular needs. See the example provided.

NAME	pitch identification	rhythmic reading example #1 (4/4)	rhythmic reading example #2 (cut time)	strum rhythm #1	strum rhythm #2	hands?

Figure 5.1   Sample audition results sheet

ASSIGNING PERSONNEL TO INSTRUMENTS

Initially, it is important to assign each member to only one instrument so they can begin developing proficiency on that particular instrument, though it can be advantageous when personnel can perform on more than one instrument type eventually. Such mobility allows players to gain a deeper understanding of how ensemble music fits together. For example, a bass pan player who learns to play lead pan as a secondary instrument will learn to function in the band as a melodic performer, as opposed to a musician who provides the bass line.

Additionally, a person who learns to play more than one type of pan is simply well rounded. Players with broader experience will take that advantage with them if they move on to a steel band experience at a different level or a different institution. Finally, a player who can perform on multiple instrument types can substitute for absent players in more situations, given his proficiency on diverse instruments.

Some directors may require that all members in the steel band develop proficiency on multiple instruments (or even all of the representative instrument types in their band), while others may leave the decision up to the players themselves. Again, it is a question of mission. In any case, keep in mind that players perhaps need not develop equal proficiency on several instrument types; rather, it may suffice for members to simply experience, even on a limited basis, performing on multiple instrument types.

Initial Assignments

Directors should consider several factors when assigning personnel to their initial or primary instrument. For one, some steel band instruments require more manual dexterity than others. In particular, those people assigned to play the "front line" voices—namely lead, double tenor, or double second pan—need to have (or be able to readily develop) the manual dexterity needed to play melodic passages. Percussionists learn to hold and to manipulate various types of beaters as a matter of course. Anyone coming to a steel band who has a percussion background will likely adapt to holding and manipulating pan mallets very well.

However, it is not essential for prospective steel band members to have a background in percussion. Players in the "low end" of the band—guitar/cello and basses—do not need to possess the same degree of dexterity that percussionists have. Considering a prospective member's hands when making initial assignments makes the learning process easier for students and the director, and reduces the necessity for switching instruments to better match players' capabilities.

Secondly, strumming does not come easily to most players, so usually only a select few individuals among the pool of members can easily demonstrate this ability. Players who are assigned to chording instruments (such as the double second or guitar/cello pan) need to capably and steadily perform syncopated strumming rhythms. Remember to test for this ability when auditioning personnel (see Holding Auditions, above). If you don't use auditions to determine personnel, then you will have to devote some time in the first rehearsal to evaluate players' ability to strum. Simply have everyone in the band take turns learning to strum a simple chord progression, and evaluate them accordingly.

Another factor to consider is clef inclination. Bass pans and guitar/cello pans are bass clef instruments, while double second pans, double tenor pans, and lead pans are treble clef instruments. If the ensemble is going to read music notation, then a director may have to consider that some members will have experience reading only in one clef. For example, a student who plays tuba in the high school marching band may read only bass clef. It would make sense to assign such a student to a pan that plays in bass clef.

Lastly, a director may find that members are most satisfied with their initial assignment if they have at least some input in the decision-making process. So, ask them! A new steel band member may have a gut reaction or a hunch as to what instrument may suit his or her personality, so to speak. For whatever reason, it may not be possible for you to assign them to their first-choice instrument, but at least you can give them a chance to have a say.

Remember, it is not advisable to have all of the best musicians in one section, at the expense of other sections. When making initial assignments, directors must ensure that they distribute strong personnel evenly throughout the ensemble.

Having More Personnel Than Instruments

In some cases, having more players than pans can actually be desirable. First, admitting extra personnel into the steel band program means that more people can participate in the activity. Second, having additional players can allow for either multiple ensembles or for personnel substitutions within a single ensemble. Either way, the director can usually pursue a greater amount of repertory under such conditions.

Another benefit of having extra personnel in a steel band that directors may not consider at first is that having multiple players assigned to each instrument decreases the odds that absences will negatively affect performances. Small steel bands benefit especially from extra players. A six-piece band, for example, with two players missing and no one to cover the parts may not be able to effectively perform their repertoire.

Having more players than instruments can pose difficulties, however, particularly when splitting the players into separate ensembles is not an option. For instance, if a school-based band meets as a class, extra personnel can cause classroom management problems to arise. Directors faced with these circumstances may turn to various solutions. A commonly employed tactic is to have partners assigned to each instrument. When one of the pair is rehearsing, the other can shadow him, observing over his shoulder. The director can have the partners swap roles frequently throughout the rehearsal, keeping both parties engaged and accountable for learning material.

Alternatively, the members can play in the rhythm section whenever they are not playing a pan, but this solution is not ideal because not every member in the ensemble has the ability to play rhythm section instruments effectively. Once again, the particular mission of the steel band rears its head! A director may decide, for instance, that he wants all of his members to learn the basic techniques of the rhythm section instruments, whether they can play them successfully in performance or not. In this case, having the personnel rotate into the rhythm section whenever they are unoccupied makes complete sense. Such a rotation keeps idle hands busy during rehearsals; in performance, the director can simply select the most capable players to perform in the rhythm section, while others sit out.

Personnel in the Engine Room

The rhythm section of a steel band is called the "engine room"; it comprises a drumset, augmented by various Latin percussion instruments selected according to whatever style of music the band is performing. Engine room players are of particular concern because they provide the underlying groove of the music. Thus, if the members of the engine room—particularly the drumset player— cannot keep time and play the groove effectively, then the music (and the audience) suffers.

Two different methods can determine engine room personnel. One involves rotating all members of the ensemble through the rhythm section at various times. Useful when players outnumber pans, this strategy places anyone not playing pan on a particular tune into the rhythm section. As a result, all members are involved

in music making at all times. What's more, each member partici-
pates in the engine room, plays those instruments, and faces the
challenges associated with them. Of course, playing the drumset
requires much more coordination than playing a simple rhythmic
ostinato on the conga drums or the shaker, so directors should not
expect every member to sit in the drumset chair.

In a second method, the director identifies key members who
can play the drumset and other percussion instruments and assigns
them exclusively to duties in the engine room. By doing so, the director creates two constituencies within the ensemble: personnel
in the engine room don't play pan, and pan players don't play in the
engine room.

The exclusivity created by this method may not appeal to educators because it does not allow everyone in the ensemble to experience playing in the engine room. However, having a solid engine
room is vital. If engine room players can't perform the groove capably, then pan players can't play their parts well either. The
rhythm section is the foundation of the music. For this reason, it
must comprise capable personnel during performances. In fact,
steel band directors themselves should be prepared to play in the
engine room at any time, in order to provide a reliable presence
and steady timekeeping. Directors should even prepare themselves for the possibility of having to play the drumset, in the event
that no one in the ensemble demonstrates that ability.

THE ADVANTAGES OF A FEEDER GROUP

When starting a steel band from the ground up, everyone involved
enters the experience as a beginner. However, even after a short
time (say, one semester) those members will have developed a basic level of proficiency. At this point, a new class of beginners
entering the ensemble would be forced to function alongside already proficient members. As time passes in the life of the band,

this gap only would become greater. Imagine a high school steel band that comprises members who have been playing pan for over three years as well as beginners who may have never seen the instruments before. These two groups have vastly different needs and expectations. In some cases the dissonance between them can become untenable. It's time, then, to develop a feeder band.

Having a tiered steel band program that teaches beginners separately from experienced players allows beginners to discover the instruments in their own time and in their own way. They can learn the basics of their instruments without pressure from others ahead of them. The beginner's ensemble is a training experience with the primary goal of exposing new members to the basic techniques and concepts of playing in a steel band. These players can then feed into the advanced ensemble.

Keep in mind that having two distinct steel band groups as described above does not mean having tiered ensembles in the traditional sense. For example, the tiered wind band situation common to many schools is not parallel to the dual steel band setup. Many high school music programs have different levels of wind band, with the understanding that only the best players are admitted into the top band, usually through an audition. The lower wind band is made up of students with lesser ability. Still, these lesser-ability students come to the experience already knowing how to play a given wind instrument. Anyone directing a steel band must keep in mind that players entering the program are coming in cold to learn a new instrument. Ability and musicianship aside, such orientation takes time. A beginner's ensemble is the best environment for beginners.

6

REPERTOIRE

For the steel band director, repertoire is virtually boundless. The only limitations are rehearsal time and the collective ability of the ensemble members. A steel band can realize practically any style of music, so directors can freely choose repertoire that is in line with their specific mission for the ensemble. The following suggestions show how to approach the selection and dissemination of repertoire.

ROTE VERSUS NOTE

Steel band directors can use either rote teaching or music notation, either exclusively or in combination. Each method of transmitting repertoire has advantages and disadvantages. In certain situations, one method might be preferable, but in the final analysis, a director must face the "rote versus note" question in the context of his or her own mission or goals for the ensemble.

Rote for Beginners

Rote teaching in the steel band can have enormous value, particularly for beginners. Most people who participate in steel band come to the ensemble with no prior experience in playing pan; rather, the ensemble setting is by and large where people first encounter the instrument. The first few rehearsals for a group of beginners can be somewhat daunting, as they try to make music happen while at the same time acclimating themselves to a completely unfamiliar instrument. Remember, even a person who has prior musical training or experience will have as much difficulty in attempting to read music notation as a neophyte pan player, for two reasons.

First, the person does not know where the pitch areas are on the instrument, and thus even though they know what pitch to play, they can't readily find it on the instrument. The pitch layouts on pans seemingly defy logic and can compound frustration: the pitch areas are not arranged in a sequential order (as in, low pitches on the left progressing to high pitches on the right, like a keyboard), thus players cannot readily intuit where a pitch area "should" be located.

Second, pan is similar to percussion keyboard instruments such as the marimba or xylophone in that the player does not touch the actual instrument with his or her hands when playing. As a result, looking at the instrument is extremely helpful in ensuring accuracy. A flute player, for instance, doesn't need to look at his flute to accurately press down the keys—he can feel where his fingers are supposed to go. However, a beginning pan player who is trying to read music notation will have a tough time keeping her eyes on the music, as she constantly puts her head down to locate the pitch area that she must strike.

For these reasons, rote teaching with beginners is the best method. Even for a director who desires to use notation in the long term, teaching beginners by rote has its advantages. At this stage, rote learning allows the beginners to spend a large portion of their mental energy simply focusing on the instrument: the location of the pitch areas, the specific elements of basic technique, and the touch required to produce good tone. A player reading notation must spend a considerable amount of energy interpreting those visual symbols and translating them into physical action. Only an experienced, highly capable musician can read notation and still have enough mental energy remaining for all of the music-making skills that ensemble playing requires.

I strongly recommend that directors employ rote teaching for beginning steel band members, at least until the players can demonstrate a rudimentary understanding of their instrument.

Rote Teaching: Other Situations

Sometimes, the membership of a steel band may comprise individuals with little or no prior musical training. In such cases, you may decide to use rote teaching exclusively. You might not want to spend time teaching members the skill of realizing printed music, for various reasons. You may simply not have the time to do so, or the players themselves may be resistant. No matter what the reason, music notation is just not for everyone.

Actually, rote learning has several advantages. For one, rote learning allows players to focus more attention on their instrument than does reading notation. Furthermore, rote learning causes players to internalize music in ways that reading notation does not. Specifically, rote learning *requires* memorization. A player who is able to proficiently read music notation may never fully internalize their music by committing it to memory; as a result, one could argue that a player who learns material by rote can actually perform the material better, because he or she performs it from memory. Most concert soloists memorize their repertoire (even though they undoubtedly *learn* the music first by reading it); if it's good enough for them, then why not encourage memorization for the steel band? Memorization is an inherent result of the rote learning process.

Using a rote method of imparting repertoire can provide the steel band members with a window into the Trinidadian culture— the source culture of this wonderful instrument. Even today, many bands in Trinidad learn repertoire by rote. Doing so does not in any way diminish these bands' abilities or achievements. Rote learning is simply part of the Trinidadian music-culture. Requiring a band that normally reads notation to learn, say, at least one arrangement by rote for a performance gives them an appreciation for how others learn music.

THE ADVANTAGES OF NOTATION

Using notation has its advantages as well. The greatest and most obvious benefit of notation is efficiency: a band can digest large amounts of material in a short time using notation. Conversely, a director that relies purely on rote teaching has to make a sacrifice. He must either choose very easy repertoire, thereby facilitating learning and memorization, or he must protract the learning process (in the case of longer, more challenging pieces). A band that can read can do a wide variety of music with less preparation time.

The availability of published arrangements and compositions is a second advantage. Thanks to the rise in steel band publishing over the past fifteen years, a band that learns music almost exclusively from notation already has a body of repertoire from which to choose. Of course, directors can still do their own arrangements, but by utilizing published music, the director does not *need* to spend time crafting arrangements. Steel band directors starting out these days have a definite advantage over their counterparts from the 1970s, when the idiom was first taking a firm hold in the United States. At that time, virtually no publishing houses dedicated to steel band literature existed, and so having composition or arranging skills as a director was a must.

DOING YOUR OWN ARRANGEMENTS

In the early days of steel band, arrangements were essential because no one had created original music for the instrument. Even today, with excellent composers writing idiomatically for pan, doing one's own arrangements still has its advantages. First, no one knows a band like its own director. Some publishers of steel band music provide difficulty ratings for the pieces in their catalogs, in the manner of wind band or choral literature. However, these ratings are inherently subjective. By doing your own arrangements, you can tailor the pieces to the ability level (not to mention the instrumentation) of your band.

Although the number of published pieces for steel band has increased dramatically over the past two decades, there is still a dearth of quality, published steel band music. Directors with active programs may find that their band's ability to learn repertoire outpaces the pan world's ability to produce new, interesting pieces.

Publishing steel band music today is not very viable from a financial standpoint because demand is so low. In order for publishers to take the financial risk of expanding their catalogs, the number of steel bands must greatly increase, thereby raising the demand for sheet music. Until that time, directors who have the ability to arrange their own music can devise effective programs without having to rehash material from a few years ago.

VARIETY: THE SPICE OF LIFE

All calypso and soca makes Jack a dull pan player. In other words, exposing your band members to a variety of musical styles makes them well-rounded musicians. An analogy: a piano teacher would never allow his students to study and perform only Bach fugues. Rather, he would make sure that the student experienced repertoire from different time periods and diverse musical genres. In the same way, steel band directors must not get caught in the trap of playing only fast, loud, exciting calypsos. Of course, calypso is a staple of the repertoire, and performing calypso pays due homage to the Trinidadian origins of pan. However, a band that plays expressive ballads and jazzy sambas for example, along with their fun calypso charts, will likely mature faster than a band that does not.

For educators, the steel band represents an excellent opportunity for teaching style differences; the steel band experience can serve as an educational lab where students learn how to realize the different challenges of performing diverse styles of music. What's more, steel band is typically so much fun that students clamor to be included. With such an energetic membership, directors in school settings should have no problem selling various genres of music to their students. Think of the possibilities: a ballad can help students develop a sensitive touch on the instruments; an arrangement of a Mozart serenade can teach listening and other "ensemble" issues; an up-tempo soca can make students aware of the powerful impact of popular music on an audience; the list could go on and on.

In the end, directors choose repertory based on several factors: the ability level of the players, the use of either rote teaching or written notation, and of course their particular mission for the ensemble. These factors aside, it behooves all directors to follow the principle of variety in selecting repertoire, no matter what their situation.

TO PANORAMA, OR NOT TO PANORAMA?

Panorama, Trinidad's annual competition for steel band, produces some of the best music for the idiom. Unfortunately, most of these arrangements are lost because the arrangers normally do not work from notated scores, though some Panorama transcriptions are available through select publishers.

For those of us who do not have the opportunity to play in the actual Panorama competition (99 percent of all pan players in the world), playing a Panorama transcription can be viewed as the height of achievement—for many, no other repertoire in the realm of pan brings as much reward or excitement. The question is: is it worth the cost? Any band wishing to realize a full-length Panorama competition transcription will need to devote a large amount of rehearsal time to the project, as Panorama music is extremely challenging to perform. Keep in mind that in Trinidad, Panorama music is played by culture members who have, in most cases, years upon years of experience playing pan. In contrast, most bands outside of Trinidad are composed of people with comparatively little (perhaps two to three years) experience.

In other words, when a band of average-ability players attempts to tackle an extraordinarily difficult piece, such as a Panorama transcription, they may have to sacrifice other repertoire. However, realizing a Panorama transcription can be a thrilling experience (for performers and audiences alike), and the band members can use the piece as a window into another music-culture. The question becomes one of balance—a band that tackles full-length Panorama transcriptions often risks becoming one-dimensional. As an alternative, directors should consider *Panorama-style* pieces; these compositions or arrangements capture the vibe of Panorama, but are less difficult and lengthy than actual transcriptions. They allow directors to expose their players to the style of Panorama music without spending an inordinate amount of time on a single piece.

COMBINING PAN WITH OTHER PERFORMING FORCES

Using pan in combination with other performing forces can be a wonderful way to add variety to programming. In the first place, a director may decide to present a combined concert of say, steel band and jazz ensemble, where each ensemble simply plays its own repertoire. This concert strategy can particularly benefit young steel bands who have not yet built up an extensive repertoire. Given this situation, you can imagine a horn player or two from the jazz ensemble playing as featured soloists along with the steel band, or even a pan soloist playing as a featured guest with the jazz ensemble.

Of course, a combined concert featuring two or more ensembles need not be a prerequisite for featuring guest soloists in the steel band. In fact, the steel band can incorporate non-pan instruments or vocalists at any time. In doing so, several advantages come to mind. First, the steel band can serve as a vehicle for soloists to shine. A steel band in a school setting, for instance, can be a second outlet (other than jazz band) for non-pan-playing students to present improvised solos. Keep in mind that featured soloists could come from outside the steel band (in a school setting, say, from one's concert band), or also from within. If one of your double second players, for example, also happens to be a really hot alto saxophone player, why not let him play the sax on a tune or two?

Second, featuring non-pan instruments or vocals on your steel band concert breaks up the timbre spectrum a bit: rather than subjecting your audience to an hour of nothing but pan, you can pepper your program with other sounds as you incorporate guest musicians. Adding vocalists can be particularly effective, as they add the element of text to the music.

Third, incorporating non-pan-performing forces into your steel band can be an opportunity to expose both the band members and audiences alike to professional-level, invited guest artists. Interaction between esteemed guest artists and your band members can be quite rewarding, so if financial resources allow, make it a habit to invite professional musicians to play with your ensemble.

Some publishing houses dedicated to steel band music offer arrangements that incorporate other instruments or vocal parts. This does not preclude directors from creating arrangements in-house that suit their own situations. Even when working from published steel band arrangements, directors can incorporate horn soloists, for example, by simply providing them with the lead pan part, and having them double the melodic line. Of course, such cases require transposition, since pans read at concert pitch. The director could easily create a transposed part for the horn soloist if the player cannot transpose at sight.

THE CASE FOR ORIGINAL MUSIC

Programming original music composed for steel band is one of the most important things a director can do. Too often, steel band directors focus on arrangements exclusively, and neglect original compositions for pan entirely. Unfortunately, if bands avoid performing original compositions, then composers have little impetus to create new pieces. Several reasons exist as to why steel band has yet to be universally recognized as a legitimate, viable art form, and the lack of a sizable body of excellent, canonical repertoire is one of them.

Consider music for winds: wind ensemble directors don't need to rely on arrangements when they have Grainger, Persichetti, and Sousa. Of course, not all wind band directors at every level are performing the classic examples of wind band literature, but the fact remains that such classics exist. It is imperative that steel band directors identify iconic composers and excellent examples of their writing, and subsequently introduce their bands to such compositions.

Every steel band director has some responsibility for the growth of pan as an idiom. Besides, composers like Ray Holman, Tom Miller, Andy Narell, and Len "Boogsie" Sharpe, to name a few, deserve to have their music played and heard. These composers have a proven track record of writing superb music for pan. A director who does not program original compositions (whenever possible;

granted, it is difficult to find many examples of excellent original works written for beginner or lower-level bands) not only cheats his members out of the experience of playing great music, but he does a disservice to pan writ large.

EDUCATE YOUR AUDIENCE!

A good strategy in terms of repertoire is to educate one's audience. Simply put, if a steel band always presents concerts that feature the same, tired repertoire with no variation in style, or with no nod to excellent original music by outstanding composers, then that band trains its audience to have very low expectations. The general public already expects little from pan, perhaps because it is an instrument that arose from the lower-class members of a third-world island nation.

Furthermore, listeners commonly (and, some would say, unfortunately) associate a standard slate of tunes like "Mary Ann," "Yellowbird," and "Day-O" with the steel band experience. A director who exclusively performs music of this ilk only contributes to the notion that pan is an instrument with limited capabilities. Instead, directors must create varied, interesting programs that showcase the wonderful versatility of pan. By doing so, we educate our audiences to expect great things from steel band, both at our own local level and in general.

I don't want to give the impression that pan should abandon its novel repertoire altogether. Steel band audiences primarily want to be entertained, and if novelty pieces get the job done, so be it. However, constantly catering to the audience leads to stagnation on both sides: audiences don't grow in terms of their appreciation for pan, and band members don't mature as musicians. Thus, the answer lies in pursuing a balanced approach to repertoire. Audiences will expect excellence only if we make an effort to show them just how excellent steel band can be.

⑦

BASIC PAN TECHNIQUE

Even for a beginner, producing a sound on a pan is nearly effortless: one merely strikes a pitch area with a mallet. However, players must realize that simply producing a sound on the instrument constitutes only the smallest, initial step in developing proficiency. Pan suffers from two fundamental misperceptions. The commonly used designation *steel drum* often causes the uninitiated to envision an actual *drum*, and of course everyone knows what we do with drums: we hit them, with great exuberance and force! A widely held misconception about drumming suggests that anyone can do it, because it takes no special skill to play a drum, or at least not as much skill as required by a wind, string, or keyboard instrument. Of course, nothing could be further from the truth.

Secondly, pans have had a novel appeal for years, due to their common association with the Caribbean and its relaxed, "fun-in-the-sun" image. As a result, people who approach the instruments can casually dismiss technique development as unnecessary. In fact, the idea that you can play pans either well or poorly, as with *any* instrument, may never enter some people's minds. Players, and especially directors, must not undervalue (or at worst, ignore altogether) technique development, because it plays an essential part of learning to play pan.

GETTING STARTED

The first step toward proficiency on any instrument simply requires becoming familiar with its capabilities. In most steel band programs with constant personnel turnover, the playing surfaces of the pans are labeled, so that beginners can learn the various pitch locations. However, you should encourage players to develop their familiarity

FAQ: Can I transfer exercises that I already use with my other ensemble(s) to the steel band?

A steel band director working in a school setting already has a battery of exercises or activities that are used with other, more traditional ensembles such as choir or band. You can readily adapt such pedagogical elements to the steel band setting. In fact, commonly used exercises can often be beneficial to pan players (especially beginners) on multiple levels. Scale exercises, for example, allow pan players to become familiar with the locations of pitch areas on the face of the instrument as well as giving players the opportunity to work on basic tone production.

Some elements may be transferable to the steel band setting, albeit used for different goals. For instance, reading simple chorales with a wind band can improve intonation and balance, but in a steel band you may employ chorales to improve the ensemble's sight-reading skill. In any case, directors should take advantage of already existing exercises, adapting them to fit the particular needs of the steel band.

with the instrument to the point that such labels are unnecessary. Exercises and activities common to other types of instruments and ensembles such as scales, arpeggios, and sight reading can certainly increase a player's comfort level with the instrument, particularly if you regularly incorporate such activities into your rehearsals.

You should also consider including unstructured discovery time as part of the technique development process. Players typically encounter pan in an ensemble setting, and as a result often only spend time with the instrument in a highly structured, corporate environment. Directors should allow for a certain amount of free time within the rehearsal setting, so that players have an opportunity to get to know the instrument individually. Significant discoveries can occur during such unstructured time, as players explore the nuances of their instrument at their own pace and direction.

SETUP AND POSTURE

As with many other percussion instruments, the position of the instrument and the relationship of the body to the instrument directly affect a player's ability to perform comfortably. In positioning pans, height is of primary concern. Players should not have to raise their shoulders in reaching over the near rim of the instrument in order to play the pitches located close to that rim. Having to do so indicates that the pans are positioned too high. On the other hand, pans that are placed too low cause the player to be constantly bent over the instrument. To avoid strain and fatigue, players should not have to bend over significantly, nor should they have to fully extend their arms, in order to reach the instrument.

Players should stand in the center of their instrument setup, with feet placed slightly apart and body weight evenly distributed. On instruments such as the lead or the double second, players should not have to move out of their stance to play. However, on instruments that comprise three or more barrels, such as triple guitars, four-cellos, or basses, foot movement may be required in order to reach all regions of the instrument. In these cases, adopting a central position with weight evenly distributed between both feet allows for maximum mobility.

HOLDING THE MALLETS

When teaching players how to hold pan mallets for the first time, it is best to allow the players to do what comes naturally, and then merely point out habits to avoid. Here are a few fundamental elements of holding the mallets:

- The pointer finger should not point down the shaft of the mallet. Such behavior causes the player to apply unnecessary pressure when stroking a note; as a result, the player may not rebound the mallet after the attack of the stroke. Failing to rebound immediately does not allow the pan to resonate freely, as it is designed to do.
- When holding the mallets used on lower voices (such as guitar pan, cello pans, or bass pans), players must become comfortable in having all of the fingers in contact with the mallet. For guitar and cello pan mallets, the pinkie finger is located very near the end of the mallet shaft.
- When holding mallets for the upper voices (lead pan, double tenor pan, double second pan), be careful not to choke up too far on the mallets. The mallets used for the upper voices have very short shafts, and choking up too far inhibits the stroke. Players may find that they only use their thumb and first two fingers to grasp the mallet. This is fine, as long as the remaining two fingers stay "in place"—that is, the two remaining fingers should be curved into the hand as if the shaft of the mallet was actually long enough to be grasped by all the fingers.

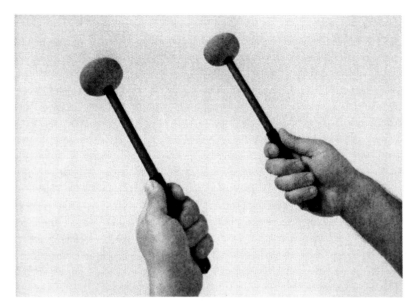

Figure 7.1a   Holding bass pan mallets

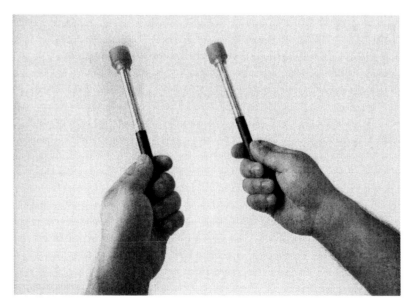

Figure 7.1b   Holding guitar/cello pan mallets

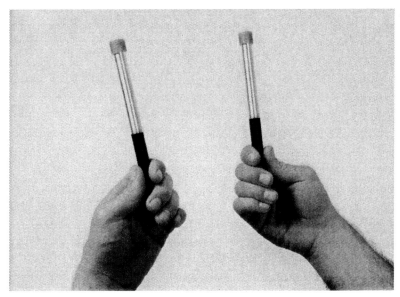

Figure 7.1c   Holding lead pan mallets

- Always avoid squeezing or gripping pan mallets too hard. Doing so can inhibit the tone of the instrument.

MECHANICS OF TECHNIQUE: HAND POSITIONS
AND STROKE MOTIONS

Two elements of technique that may be called "mechanics" are
hand positions relative to the instrument and stroke motions. It is
important to understand that pans are unique percussion instruments because their playing surfaces are concave, as opposed to
flat. The curved nature of the playing surface has ramifications for
both hand positions and also for the manner in which players execute effective strokes.

Hand Positions

Players should learn two basic hand positions. Let us call these two positions "above the rim" (see figure 7.2) and "below the rim" (see figure 7.3). Imagine that the circular playing surface of a barrel is divided into halves: one half is near to the player, and the other half is far from the player. When striking areas on the near half of the pan, the hands should remain above the plane of the rim, and when striking areas on the far half, the hands move to a position inside the bowl (or below the rim). Learning to place one's hands in these two appropriate positions allows players to move their hands around the concave surface of the instrument with the most efficiently, with as little arm movement as possible.

One of the most common errors that inexperienced players make is leaving their hands in the "above the rim" position when striking areas on the far half of the instrument (see figure 7.4). This action forces them to lift their arms high, and possibly even to hold their arms at uncomfortable angles. Placing one's hands below the rim, and thus actually inside the bowl of the pan, when striking these pitch areas allows players to maintain a relaxed, comfortable upper-body posture. Of course, rules have exceptions; for instance, the player may find it advisable to place his or her hands in an unconventional position in certain passages involving pitch areas within a limited area of the instrument. Nonetheless, these two hand positions should be taught and learned as the basic, default positions to adopt.

Lastly, pitch areas that fall on the imaginary boundary line that divides the near half and the far half of the pan (such as the pitches A and E-flat on a circle-of-fifths lead pan) present a gray area when applying these hand positions. Which hand position to use when playing these pitch areas is a judgment call: it depends on the passage being performed, and thus what other pitch areas are also involved in the execution of that passage.

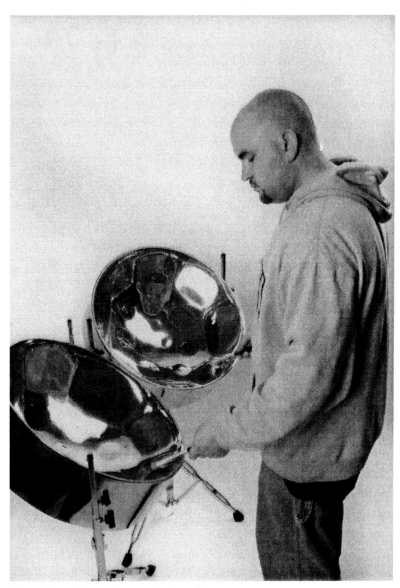

Figure 7.2   Above the rim hand position

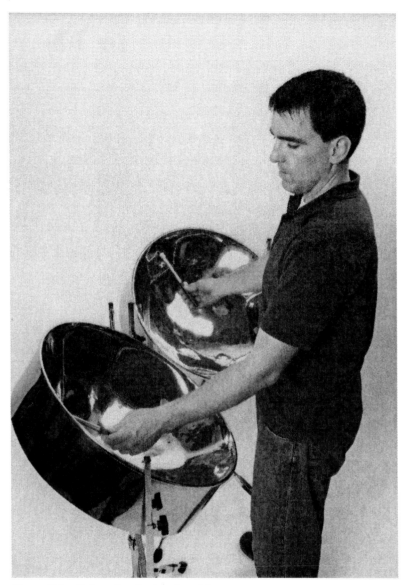

Figure 7.3   Below the rim hand position

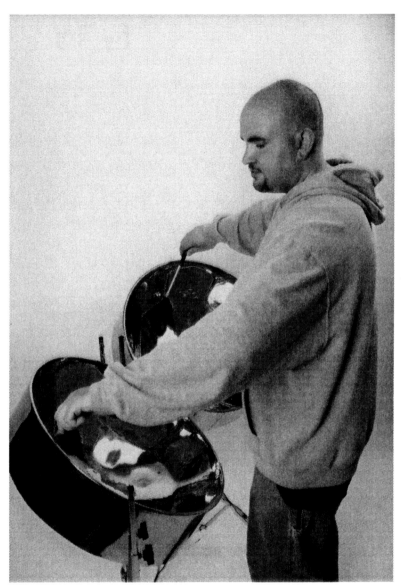

Figure 7.4   Poor hand position

Stroke Motions

Again, the concave surface of pans means that players must adopt several different types of stroke in order to effectively negotiate the various pitch areas on a given instrument. There are three stroke motions.

Basic Stroke

With the basic stroke, the pan player uses a technique common to many percussion instruments. With the palm facing down, the player simply executes a vertical motion to strike a pitch area. The basic stroke is perhaps the most commonly used stroke.

Side Stroke

This type of stroke is used to strike a pitch area that is on the side of the bowl. With the palm oriented downward, the hand moves to the side, away from the body. Using a side stroke usually allows the player to keep the hands in a good, relaxed position relative to the instrument, as opposed to moving the arm into an awkward position and trying to use the basic stroke to hit a pitch area on the side of the bowl.

Sweep Stroke

The "sweep" can be a most effective stroke technique, particularly when executing passages with rapid note values, or when executing passages involving pitch areas on opposite sides of the face of the pan. The sweep stroke is used to quickly and efficiently traverse the distance between two areas: a "doorknob" or rotating wrist stroke is used to move the mallet from one area to another, rather than using the arm to move the mallet (the arm is larger than the wrist, so it moves more slowly and less efficiently). In utilizing the sweep stroke, players must learn to place their hand in between the two pitch areas. The sweep stroke technique takes some getting used to, and players need constant reminders to apply it.

PRODUCING A GOOD TONE

Three different ingredients produce a good tone: using the correct part of the mallet end to strike the pan, finding the sweet spot for each pitch area, and developing touch.

The Mallet: A Closer Look

Pan mallets designed for guitar/cello pans, double second or double tenor pans, or lead pans are typically made with varying thicknesses of rubber tubing on the end. When striking a pan, one should avoid doing so with the flat side of this rubber tubing (see figure 7.5). Doing so produces an unpleasant "splat" at the front of the sound. Rather, players should endeavor to strike each pitch area with the corner of the mallet end, at the edge of the rubber tubing (see figure. 7.6). Using the edge of the tubing to strike the instrument produces a warm tone with little attack sound.

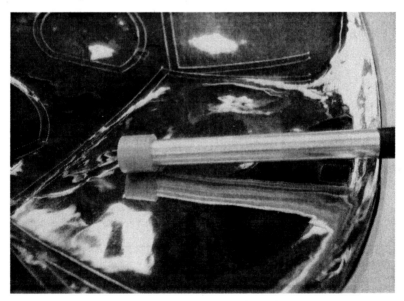

Figure 7.5   Striking a pan with the flat side of a mallet

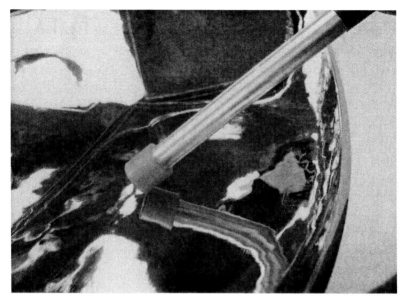

Figure 7.6   Striking a pan with the edge of the mallet

The Sweet Spot

Pan players soon discover that merely striking their instrument anywhere within the boundary of a particular pitch area does not guarantee a good tone quality. Players must develop a sense of where the sweet spot is for every pitch area on their instrument. Typically, the best sound on any given pitch area arises when the player strikes the center of the pitch area. In crafting a pan, a tuner places the fundamental tone of a pitch in the central region of the given pitch area. As a result, striking a pitch area outside its center often produces too much overtone sound, and not enough of the fundamental.

When players can see where their mallets are striking, they can make sure that they hit the centers of each pitch area. As soon as players focus their attention to printed music (taking their eyes off the pans), consistently striking the sweet spots of pitch areas becomes quite difficult, especially for beginners. Like percussion keyboard instruments such as the marimba or xylophone, pan presents a challenge to players in that the instrument is non-tactile: players do not touch the instrument itself when playing. As a result, accuracy is usually improved if the player looks at the instrument. Obviously players cannot look at the instrument if they are reading music notation, so directors may want to encourage memorization if the ensemble learns music primarily through notation.

Developing Touch

Developing a sensitive touch on pans is one of the most challenging aspects of the technique. On any given pan, the various sizes of pitch areas each correspond to a different pitch. Smaller areas create higher pitches than larger areas do. The smaller areas (higher pitches) require more force to speak than the larger areas (lower pitches). This means that a player must strike pitch areas with different amounts of force in order to create an equal dynamic across the range of the instrument.

Consider this example: a player needs to execute a two-octave, descending arpeggio, with all pitches sounding at mezzoforte. The player would need to strike the upper pitches of the arpeggio with more force than the lower pitches in order to achieve this result. Striking the higher pitches too softly does not make them speak well enough; conversely, striking the lower pitches with too much force causes an unpleasant tone, and possibly an out-of-tune pan. Newcomers to steel drum instruments must be educated in this aspect of technique early in their development.

PLAYING ROLLS

Rolling is a way for a pan player to simulate a sustained sound. Of course, a true sustained tone cannot be achieved, because the player is not using breath or a bow, for example. However, the sound of a roll should come as close as possible to a true sustained tone. As with percussion keyboard instruments such as the marimba, all rolls on pans are to be executed as single-stroke rolls, meaning players should not bounce the mallets multiple times for each stroke. Another comparison to the marimba applies: smaller pitch areas on pans (like the smaller bars on a marimba) require a faster roll speed than do larger pitch areas in order to achieve a sustained sound.

Not only are different roll speeds appropriate on any given pan, they also apply from one instrument type to another. In fact, it is generally true that all of the pitch areas on the double second pan require a faster roll speed than any of the pitch areas on the bass pans.

Many times, players new to pans experience difficulty in developing roll technique, because their hand speed is often not fast enough to produce the illusion of a sustained sound. As a result, their rolls sound too measured or rhythmic. When a criticism of slow roll speed is leveled at such a player, his natural reaction causes him to try and increase the speed; this invariably produces tension in the player's body, and results in a poor tone quality—or it results in barely any tone produced at all, as the player "locks up" in his struggle to rapidly stroke the roll. A player who tries to achieve a fast roll speed too soon in his development will never improve upon this challenging aspect of technique. Instead, the player should be instructed to continue playing rolls using only the fastest speed he can achieve while still maintaining a relaxed approach to the instrument. By doing so, his hand speed will improve and increase over time. In the meantime, the utilization of a slow roll speed at least produces a tone on the pan, and for that matter, the player's slow roll speed blends into the overall sound of the section.

Unfortunately, not all published steel band music indicates where rolls are to be used. In a band setting, it is important for the director to study the score prior to rehearsal, using his or her own discretion to determine where to use rolls. In this way, the director can ensure consistency in articulation among all members of a section.

CHOOSING STICKINGS

Choosing stickings refers to the process of deciding which hand to use in executing the various notes of a passage. For an experienced player, choosing stickings is an intuitive process that often happens "on the fly," as the player performs a passage. However, for a beginning or even an intermediate player, working out sticking patterns prior to rehearsal or performance has enormous value. A director might encourage ensemble members to write in stickings below the part, so that they will not have to waste valuable practice or rehearsal time relearning the stickings of challenging passages. By selecting a definitive sticking for a passage and then marrying that sticking to the pitches, a player can learn the passage more efficiently. When developing stickings, consider the following five guidelines:

1. *There is more than one acceptable way to stick a passage.*

Inexperienced players may not realize that there is usually more than one sticking solution for any given musical phrase. When such a player works out a passage, she may simply stick it according to the first way that comes to mind. As a result, her solution may not be the best one possible. Directors must often coach players in this aspect of technique so they learn to experiment with different sticking solutions.

In a band setting where there are multiple players in each section, various members of the section may arrive at different stickings, all of which are acceptable. All members of a section need not perform the exact same stickings. However, encourage communication and collaboration between members, especially between experienced and inexperienced members. Through comparison, players may find that another player's sticking works better than theirs. Beginners can certainly benefit from the expertise of experienced players in developing stickings that are both comfortable and efficient.

2. *Find the key points of the passage.*

When working out a sticking for a passage, the best practice is not always to start from the beginning of the passage and work your way through. Rather, you must begin working from key points in the passage, where you can tell with certainty what hand must be used. After determining the sticking for these key points in the passage, work either backward or forward from these points until the passage is completely solved.

3. *Know when to alternate and when to double.*

Alternating strokes (RLRL) usually produce a smooth, even sound. However, in some cases, doubling (RR or LL) makes more sense. For example, when a passage contains successive notes on one pitch, it is often advisable to play all of the notes with the same hand. However, if the rhythm is too fast, or the number of repeated notes is too numerous, then alternation may be necessary.

It is simply impossible to play any pan using alternating sticking at all times. Thus the question is not if, but how, to double. Consider several things when figuring out the best place in a passage to use double stickings. First, having equal strength and ability in both hands is an ultimate goal for all players of percussion instruments. However, not all players achieve this ideal aspect of proficiency. If a player indeed has a stronger hand, and faces a doubling choice between one hand or the other, then he will likely feel more comfortable doubling with his stronger hand.

Second, doubling between pitch areas that are physically close to each other on the surface of the pan, as opposed to pitch areas that are physically far apart, is usually easier. Also, choose to double between slower note values rather than faster ones. For instance, given three different pitches in the rhythm sixteenth-eighth-sixteenth, put the double sticking between the last two notes instead of the first two.

4. Cross if it makes a smooth musical line.

Here, "crossing" refers to positioning one's hand on the opposite side of the instrument; for example, using the left hand to strike a pitch area on the right barrel of a double tenor pan. Always keeping the hands separate (i.e., right hand covers only the right side of the instrument, left hand covers only the left side) can result in playing three or four consecutive notes with the same hand, which becomes quite difficult at fast tempi.

One school of thought instructs players to adopt a default position of keeping their hands separate as much as possible—in other words, using the left hand to play pitch areas almost exclusively on the left side of the instrument, while mirroring the behavior on the right side of the instrument. This type of instruction can actually be beneficial for beginners who may either simply make arbitrary sticking decisions, or who may favor one hand over the other without considering the position of a given pitch area on the instrument. However, encourage players to seek several solutions when a difficult passage presents itself. The more experienced a player becomes, the more easily he or she can make decisions regarding this aspect of sticking.

5. Know when to break the rules.

There is no absolute method for developing stickings. In the end, players must make decisions based on the sound that they produce, trying different stickings until they find one that allows them to produce the best tone. Bottom line: search for the best possible solution and make it work.

DEVELOPING AN IDEAL AURAL CONCEPT

Playing a musical instrument proficiently is a process that extends throughout a person's entire experience with that instrument.

Like all musicians, pan players must develop a clear mental concept of the ideal sound of their particular instrument. In order to develop this ideal aural concept, players must have models to emulate. In addition to observing the modeling provided by a teacher or director, listening to recordings or observing excellent performers firsthand are two ways that players can begin to establish an idea of what pans should sound like. Players can then compare the actual sounds they make on the instrument with their ideal aural concept, with the goal of making the actual come as close to the ideal as possible.

Such comparison and evaluation cannot take place, however, if the players do not learn to listen to themselves. The importance of developing critical listening skills cannot be taken too lightly, and thus directors must continuously remind ensemble members to be aware of their own tone production any time they approach the instrument.

8

THE ENGINE ROOM

In steel band lingo, the term *engine room* refers to the section of the band that stokes the boiler fires for the rest of the ensemble. In most other ensemble types, we use the term *rhythm section* instead. A rhythm section typically comprises the instruments that supply the chords, bass line, and rhythmic pulse. For example, the rhythm section of a jazz ensemble would include piano or guitar, bass, and drumset. However, in a steel band, the engine room is generally considered to include only the drumset and other accompanying percussion instruments; none of the pans are part of the engine room.

The primary purpose of the engine room, as with all rhythm sections, is to keep time by establishing a rhythmic undercurrent that forms the foundation of a tune. The remainder of the ensemble rides on top of this undercurrent, also known as the *groove*, in the same way that the passengers on a train ride over the tracks.

Some see the engine room as a somewhat separate section within the ensemble that has an accompanying or supporting role in the music. However, directors must not make the mistake of inadequately addressing engine room issues in rehearsal. Remember that while the rhythm section in a popular music ensemble does indeed function in a supportive role in relation to the melody instruments, at the same time it provides the very foundation of the music—the stylistic groove. As any director of a jazz band, pep band, or show choir can attest, a good groove underneath the melodic performers can make or break the gig. In other words, having excellent melody players fronting your band is great, but if the rhythm section is not hip, the music suffers.

JOB ONE: ACQUIRING STYLISTIC KNOWLEDGE

Each musical style has its own distinct groove, and any player who wants to be successful in the engine room must know the appropriate groove to play for each style. Every groove has basic, fundamental characteristics (for instance, a drummer playing a basic rock and roll groove plays the snare drum on counts two and four of a four-beat measure); a deeper knowledge of style characteristics generates a more nuanced approach to creating a groove. In many cases, steel band members come to the experience with little or no prior exposure to the styles of popular music commonly found in the repertoire (like calypso, soca, samba, reggae, salsa), so the director often serves as the primary conduit for stylistic information.

Unfortunately, the steel band director *also* often comes into the position with little or no prior exposure to these styles. Wind band, choral, and orchestra directors typically learn elements of style during their college years through ensemble participation, methods classes, and analysis courses. However, many if not most individuals directing steel bands in the United States these days did not perform in a steel band in college. Thus, it is imperative that inexperienced steel band directors take steps to acquire stylistic knowledge immediately.

You can gain such knowledge by listening to recordings and observing videos of performances involving target styles, and by reading print resources (journal articles, method books). You can attend live performances of model steel bands, and even steel band workshops. Finally, inviting guest artists or clinicians to work with you and your ensembles is extremely beneficial.

I must emphasize that nothing can substitute for seeing stylistic grooves and engine room techniques demonstrated firsthand. Remember that notation serves only as a guide for performance, and that it often fails to transmit the kind of nuance and interpretation that a performer or clinician can provide.

THE DRUMSET

The drumset is the most important instrument in the steel band rhythm section. When selecting a drummer, the director should keep in mind that keeping time is the drummer's primary duty. Flashy chops and the ability to play extended solos are not prerequisites for playing drums in the steel band; in fact, drummers of this ilk must be trained anew, and then constantly monitored (read: hounded) so as not to revert to undesirable tendencies. For the most part, a "less is more" approach to playing drumset in a steel band is the way to go.

Aside from timekeeping, the steel band drummer must take the lead in establishing the style of the music. Nothing is more irritating than listening to a drummer who plays stylistically incorrect (those who adjudicate jazz band festivals or competitions will sympathize here). For drumset players, listening to recordings provides the most practical avenue for acquiring stylistic knowledge. Directors should encourage the drummer to listen to recorded examples of music as well as play along with the recordings. Finally, whenever you program a piece and a recording of that very piece exists (not often enough, unfortunately), you should not hesitate to instruct the drummer to simply emulate the recording as closely as possible. Learning to do by first learning to mimic or imitate is one of the most tried-and-true methods of developing technique.

In addition to keeping time, the drummer can aid the navigation of a chart by delineating sections and setting up important kicks or figures, in the same way that a jazz band drummer would do. The absence of a conductor in a steel band performance makes this aspect of the drummer's job that much more significant. True, a drummer who merely plays time throughout an arrangement fulfills the fundamental requirement of his position, but a drummer who can help the band though a chart by cueing new sections or by clearly setting up syncopated hits can make the band sound tight and polished. A good drummer is not a mere timekeeping machine, but a savvy musician who has the ability to steer the group during performance.

AUXILIARY PERCUSSION IN THE ENGINE ROOM

Various auxiliary percussion instruments round out the engine room. Auxiliary percussion instruments enhance the basic groove provided by the drummer. Every steel band engine room should contain certain fundamental instruments. For directors working in a school setting, it is likely that the music program already owns most of these.

Congas
   Conga drums are perhaps the most essential engine room instrument next to the drumset. They are absolutely necessary

in certain styles such as calypso or salsa, but you can also use them in practically any style of music. You need two conga drums, tuned to relative pitches, high and low.

Bells

It's always a good idea to have a mix of different-sized cowbells available, as well as a set of ago-go bells (which are used in some Brazilian styles of music, like samba).

Shakers

As with bells, I recommend having shakers in a variety of sizes and timbres.

Scrapers

The *guiro* is important in Afro-Cuban styles of music such as the cha cha. Metal scrapers can be used for soca tunes.

Brake drum

Called an "iron" in Trinidad, an automobile brake drum is an important instrument in the realization of calypso and soca music. You can typically find brake drums at junkyards. Have your engine room members play the iron with either metal beaters or wooden drumsticks.

The preceding list comprises "must-have" items. You can add further auxiliary percussion instruments at your discretion.

Selecting Auxiliary Percussion Based on Style

One of the areas of greatest confusion for inexperienced steel band directors concerns deciding what types of auxiliary percussion instruments to use for a particular piece of music. Unfortunately, most published scores of steel band music today do not include auxiliary percussion parts. Rather, most scores include only a skeletal drumset part, similar to that of a typical jazz band chart. Publishers typically omit auxiliary percussion information for two reasons. First, additional parts translate to additional publishing costs; second, publishers assume that directors have the requisite stylistic knowledge to make informed decisions in this regard.

You should strive to achieve stylistic integrity in the engine room as much as possible. Such integrity is established both by using suitable percussion instruments in the engine room for each particular groove, and also by playing stylistically appropriate rhythmic patterns on those instruments. Again, I cannot overemphasize the importance of acquiring stylistic knowledge so that you can make informed choices regarding both of these facets of engine room management.

Musical styles are distinct from one another, and players deserve to be educated as to the specific characteristics of each style they may encounter in an ensemble. I'm not saying that there is only one way to perform each musical style. Think of it this way, for example: all jazz musicians can recognize swing when they hear it, in spite of the diversity of approaches, because they recognize certain fundamental elements of the style.

As a steel band director, you must know the fundamental elements of each musical style in your repertoire, so that you can accurately represent those styles to audiences. Again, accuracy of representation derives from selecting appropriate auxiliary percussion instruments, and then instructing players to perform appropriate rhythmic patterns on those instruments. Suggested print resources that address Latin American or Caribbean musical styles can be found in Appendix A.

Avoiding Clutter

"Avoiding clutter" refers not to the condition of your rehearsal room (although the addition of a steel band to a school music program can certainly put strains on storage space!), but rather to the condition of the groove. In order for music to achieve a good "feel," the groove must be clear. Adding excess instrumentation to the engine room can make it impossible to establish a good feel in a piece.

For example, having one student playing a shaker along with the drummer is a difficult enough proposition, since the shaker must align exactly with the drummer's groove. If the two players do not cohere, it becomes readily apparent to anyone listening critically. Considering this difficulty, the worst thing one can do is to throw in a few more shaker players! Doing so makes rhythmic alignment between these instruments virtually impossible and destroys any possibility of a clear groove. Whenever possible, directors should avoid incorporating players into the engine room just to keep them occupied. Always have a clear, musical reason for including a player into an engine room groove.

Avoiding clutter in the groove is critical for two reasons. First, the other ensemble members need a well-defined groove to lock onto. Band members rely on the rhythm section to provide a clear groove as a reference point. If the groove is unclear, the ensemble does not know which rhythmic pulse to follow. Secondly, a rhythm section that is too busy and not locked in together can distract audience members. Remember, the groove is supportive in nature—you don't want the audience focusing in on the problems in the rhythm section; rather, you want them to pay attention primarily to the rest of the ensemble. A groove is best when it enhances the music it supports, not when it distracts from it.

Groove Maintenance

Maintaining a groove as a rhythm section player is one of the most challenging things to do in an ensemble, but your members may not understand this, failing to take their role in the engine room seriously. Directors must impart to ensemble members the importance of being actively engaged at all times. When players disengage their minds from the task at hand, the potential for disaster looms. For example, a cowbell player whose mind starts to wander in the middle of a tune can wreck a groove in a few seconds, as various ensemble members decide either to follow the bell or to follow the drummer.

Let's face it: playing steady pulses on a cowbell for the entire duration of a four-minute chart may not be the most exciting activity in a person's life. Directors need to convince players that playing in the engine room is a highly important job; it is not the musical equivalent of eating leftovers. Live by this mantra: if you don't contribute to the groove, you detract from it. There is no middle ground.

A CLOSER LOOK: CALYPSO AND SOCA

Calypso and soca are two musical styles that emanate from Trinidad. Although neither was created specifically with steel bands in mind, these two styles have become part of the permanent fabric of steel band over the years, since they share a common heritage. As a result, anyone who wants to lead a steel band must become familiar with these two styles of music.

Calypso and Soca Drumset

From an ethnomusicologist's perspective, calypso and soca may be quite different, but in the steel band idiom, not much separates the two styles. In fact, the greatest difference occurs in the drumset patterns commonly performed for each style. The drumset groove for calypso features a very simple orchestration, involving only the bass drum and hi-hat:

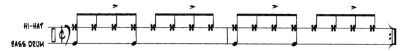

Figure 8.1   Calypso drumset groove

In contrast, the soca drumset pattern is a bit more involved:

Figure 8.2   Soca drumset groove

Aside from keeping time using these groove patterns, drumset players also have the responsibility of catching any kicks or hits with the band. Published charts that include a drumset part typically indicate these kicks, in the same way that a chart for jazz ensemble would.

Auxiliary Percussion in Calypso and Soca

The score below shows idiomatic rhythmic patterns for four instruments: congas, brake drum, shaker, and cowbell. These four instruments are all acceptable in both calypso and soca music. All four instruments do not necessarily need to be used in every piece of calypso or soca music; of the four, the congas and brake drum are the most commonly used. Concerning the conga drum pattern, all strokes should be open tone strokes; no bass tones or slap tones need be used in effecting the given rhythmic pattern. In the event that performers have difficulty producing resonant, consistent sounds on the drums, soft yarn mallets or even medium-sized pan mallets (such as those used for triple guitars or four-cellos) can be used as beaters.

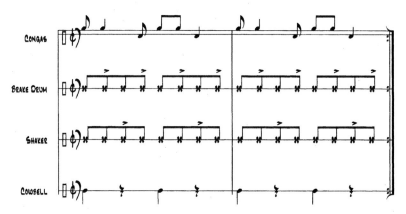

Figure 8.3   Suggested auxiliary percussion score for calypso and soca

Playing the Iron

The iron is perhaps the most defining percussion instrument in the steel band rhythm section for calypso and soca music. Light metal beaters are preferable; you can obtain them at your local hardware store. Simply ask one of the employees to cut some ¼" diameter metal rods into 10" lengths for you. If this is too much trouble, triangle beaters can do in a pinch, or you can simply use the butt ends of wooden drumsticks.

The iron usually plays a constant stream of eighth notes in cut time. The player places accents along this stream to highlight the off beats (as shown in figure 8.3). You can create accents just by using different beating spots: for the accented notes, strike the inner rim of the iron (see the left-hand position in figure 8.4), and for non-accented notes strike the surface of the iron midway between the edge and the inner rim (see the right-hand position in the photo below). You can perform many accent pattern variations on the iron, but the score above illustrates one of the most common. If a player cannot produce accents effectively while playing the iron, they can just play constant eighth notes with no accents.

The sound of the iron ringing in a steel band during a calypso or soca chart provides one of the most enchanting sounds that one

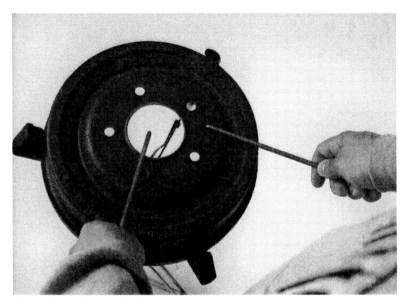

Figure 8.4   Playing the iron

can experience in this idiom. The playing of the iron raises the "happiness quotient" so much that in Trinidad, songs have been written in tribute to this seemingly lowly instrument. Don't underestimate its power. Simply put, no steel band can be without an iron.

The rhythm section of a steel band makes the music come together, so it deserves much attention. Directors and players alike must put the same amount of energy and effort into establishing the time and feel of a piece as they do in performing the melodic and harmonic instruments of the steel band. If not, the music will simply not have the element of "sweetness" that Duke Ellington described in his famous tune, "It Don't Mean a Thing If It Ain't Got That Swing." Ellington extols the great feeling that rhythm section players create for the rest of the band when they establish a groove. Be sure that your engine room, and your band, has that sweet feeling when they perform.

9

REHEARSALS AND PERFORMANCES

Unprepared steel band directors need to keep the following principle in mind: the purpose of rehearsal is to approach the ideal, perfect performance as closely as possible. To do so, one must be able to form a concept of what an ideal performance sounds like. Given their lack of preparedness, many first-time directors will have a difficult time generating such an ideal performance concept. Therefore, it is critical that directors educate themselves (and their students) by listening to model examples of Caribbean styles of music such as calypso and soca that are common to the steel band repertoire as well as model performances or recordings by established steel bands.

Before moving into a discussion of specific strategies for rehearsing a steel band, let us examine the differences between a steel band and more traditional ensembles. First, the repertoire of steel band comprises by and large popular musical styles, performed with a groove provided by a rhythm section. Such practice differs greatly from ensembles such as orchestra, wind band, or choir. The latter ensembles often perform art music, while a steel band is more akin to a rock band or a jazz ensemble, where the presence of a rhythm section eliminates the need for a conductor to provide visual cues. Second, the members of a steel band often do not read music notation during performance; even if the repertoire has been learned through notation, members often memorize it.

Third, the audience expectations of a steel band concert may be narrower. While an art music performance can entertain, other motivations may exist for witnessing such a performance: audience members may attend to hear particular repertory that they know and appreciate, or they may be in pursuit of an edifying, "artistic" experience. On the other hand, anyone coming to hear a steel band concert probably just wants entertainment. These differences in both performance practice and reception lead to rehearsal techniques and strategies for the steel band that may clash with those of traditional Western music ensembles.

SETTING UP YOUR BAND

One of the first issues to address is the rehearsal and performance setup, or the configuration of instruments in relation to one another. Small bands may not need to address this question, but as a band grows and sections begin to comprise three or more instruments, a steel band takes up a great deal of physical space. Several possible ensemble configurations exist, and directors may choose to use different ones for diverse purposes.

Grouping instruments by sections is one way of configuring your band. In this system, you place all of the instruments in a section (for example, all double second pans) together. This model still allows a number of options. For instance, the double second section might form part of a front line, or it might form a cluster on one side of the ensemble. In any case, grouping the instruments by section permits the players to hear their section's part clearly. This configuration

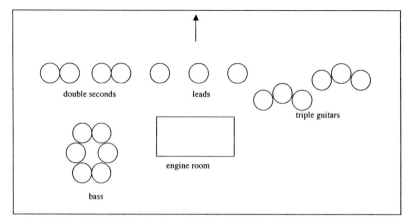

Figure 9.I   Grouping instruments by sections

works best for beginners, because the members of a section are grouped together, and can thus interact with one another readily.

A second strategy involves *not* grouping the instruments by section. In this scheme, you position diverse instrument types next to one another, so that members can hear musical parts other than their own. Such a part distribution as practiced by choirs forces the members to interact aurally with other musical lines, arguably developing the singers' intonation. Of course, intonation does not impact steel band, but this type of setup can increase a pan player's sense of ensemble awareness, which can in turn assist the director in teaching concepts such as balance or blend. Each of these strategies works well in both rehearsal and performance environments.

In a third way of setting up the pans, all players face inward in a "box" configuration. Though unacceptable for performance (as some of the players would have their backs to the audience), it can present a favorable setup for rehearsal purposes. With all players facing the center, the director can stand in the middle of the configuration, and address all members with ease. When teaching music by rote, such a setup can prove especially helpful because the director has quick access to all instruments or sections, and can move among them efficiently.

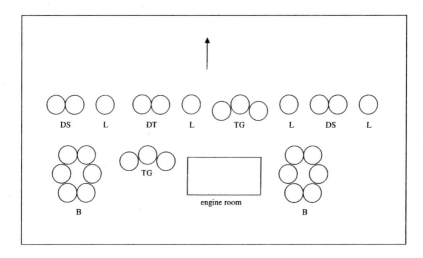

Figure 9.2   Mixed configuration

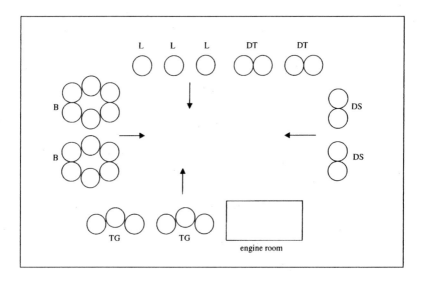

Figure 9.3   Box configuration (for rehearsals only)

One recommendation that will prove highly valuable involves the placement of the rhythm section. Inexperienced directors often place the rhythm section at the extreme rear of the ensemble setup. However, it is best to locate the rhythm section in the center of the ensemble, surrounded by pans. This setup minimizes the distance between the rhythm section and the furthest pan. Keep in mind that the rhythm section is the heart of the ensemble, musically speaking—it keeps the pulse for everyone. Thus, positioning the heartbeat of the band centrally only makes sense. Avoid placing the rhythm section at the back of the ensemble; doing so can break the connection between them and the rest of the band, spelling disaster for the groove and feel of the music.

WARMING UP

On the surface, warming up at the beginning of a steel band rehearsal may not seem as necessary as doing so in a wind band rehearsal: pan players do not need to put air through the instruments, and scale exercises or chorales are not going to help the pan players' intonation. However, you'll find a short warm-up period beneficial, albeit in different ways.

Keep in mind that by and large, pan players do not own their own instruments; furthermore, pans are not available for rental through the local music store and usually the only instruments available to the members are those that the band or institution owns. Consequently, rehearsal typically offers the only time that players actually spend on the instruments. Thus, it behooves directors to allow for a few minutes (at least) of warm up at the beginning of each rehearsal session. In addition to structured activities and exercises such as scales, arpeggios, and the like, some unstructured "noodling" may also be beneficial, particularly for inexperienced beginners, who simply need time to get to know the instrument.

FOUR IDIOMATIC REHEARSAL TECHNIQUES

The rehearsal techniques in a steel band setting may differ from those practiced by conductors of bands, orchestras, or choirs. This section addresses four specific techniques that steel band directors may choose to employ.

Going Mobile

Because she is not anchored to a podium supplying visual information during a rehearsal, the steel band director should feel free to move about the band. Traditional conductors can only dream of having such mobility. The steel band director can freely move among the ensemble, distributing individual nuggets of instruction. She can move in close to listen critically to a section while also using proximity to observe individuals and correct technique on a one-on-one basis. Such personal attention to detail can be highly advantageous, because inexperienced members require constant reminders concerning proper technique and tone production. For anyone teaching repertoire by rote, the ability to move around the band and to interact closely with individual players is essential.

Using a Time Reference

Remember, steel band music for the most part is popular music, performed to a groove provided by a rhythm section. It only makes sense in rehearsal to have a groove, or at least some reference to time, occurring. A director has several options for employing a time reference while a particular passage or section of a chart is being rehearsed:

1. The director can keep time by using a cowbell or some other appropriate hand-held percussion instrument; a pair of drumsticks struck together can also serve this function.

2. The director can instruct the drumset player to keep time by simply playing beats on the hi-hat.
3. The director can instruct the drumset player to play the groove for the band.
4. The entire rhythm section (drumset and supporting percussion instruments) can play the groove.

The first two strategies are relatively unobtrusive; they both express only the beat or pulse, allowing the director to hear the pan parts as they are rehearsed. In the latter two, the increased sound generated by either the drumset or the entire rhythm section may make listening critically more difficult for the director.

Any orchestra director worth his salt would never deign to whack a cowbell while the woodwinds rehearsed a passage, because the cowbell isn't played during the actual orchestra performance. But steel band music *is* performed to a groove (most often), so rehearsing with an overt, aural reference to time makes perfect sense for pan. The members must become accustomed to placing their parts in line with timekeeping; in other words, they must learn to hear and interact with the time.

Looping

Another rehearsal practice commonly used in steel band settings that conductors of bands, orchestras, or choirs usually avoid is the practice of looping. When using a loop, the director instructs the band to play a segment of music—a difficult lick, a phrase, or even an entire section—over and over again with only a brief break for a count-off separating each repetition. Because it is common in steel band that the members do not have the opportunity to spend time in individual practice, looping a passage helps players to solidify stickings, to become comfortable in transitions, and to strengthen muscle memory. Thus, looping replicates the kind of work that a violinist, for instance, might accomplish on her own in the practice room. When used in the context of a phrase or section, looping can be critical for establishing the *feel* of the passage—the intangible element of groove-based music that can only be developed through familiarity and repetition.

Isolating Sections, Isolating Functions

Ensemble directors commonly isolate a particular section of instruments ("May I hear all of the clarinets at letter H, please?") in rehearsals, and steel band directors can employ this technique quite effectively as well. Furthermore, it can help to isolate *functions* in the band. For example, the director may want to hear all of the melody players at once. Given that most steel band music is popular music, arrangements typically have an orchestration that features three functions: melody, chords, bass.

LEARNING TO *PERFORM*

The performance of popular music differs greatly from that of art music. In a pop music setting, audiences expect the performers to overtly demonstrate that they are having fun. On the mild side, such demonstrations could include smiling, making eye contact with the audience or with other band members, or swaying to the beat. On the bombastic side, overt demonstrations could involve jumping up and down while whooping for joy! The point is that playing pan is lots of fun, and players should make an effort to convey that enjoyment to the audience.

A steel band can have an enormous visual impact in performance, and directors should capitalize on this facet of performance. Ensemble members can express their emotions through facial expression and body movement; whether or not the band creates a visual impact can mean the difference between a good performance and a mediocre one. One of the simplest ways to get some visual excitement in the band is to have everyone move their body to the pulse; the easiest way to do this is to have everyone walk in place or tap their foot. Once the players begin to move in this way, they find that it enhances their ability to feel the groove.

Believe it or not, many people are not natural performers—they need to be coached. As a performance approaches, directors should make it a point of reminding players to stop merely playing notes and to start *performing*. Novice players may not notice the gradual change in the quality of their playing as they move from rehearsal toward performance. A director should point out when he or she actually *hears* performance-quality music.

Of course, relying solely on visual impact without bothering to coach the musical side of things is not a good tactic, and results in a feeling among the audience that the band is "all light and no heat." Making good music comes first, but an ensemble that knows how to connect with an audience and make them wish they were on stage with the band can turn a merely good performance into a memorable one.

SHOWTIME!

When it is finally time for the band to take the stage, what does the director do? It has already been established that steel bands do not typically require a director to conduct the performance; as a result, the director can actually join the ensemble and perform alongside the band members. Some directors, particularly if they own their own instrument, may choose to play pan, while others may simply elect to become a member of the rhythm section. In fact, a director who performs in the engine room can exert a measure of control over the ensemble by establishing and maintaining a steady tempo. The director can accomplish this most easily by playing a cowbell or an iron in the engine room.

A steel band performance unfolds differently than a traditional band or orchestra concert. For instance, the director should make an effort during performances to engage the audience. Even in situations where you provide a printed program, you can still announce selections from the stage. This allows you to not only establish a rapport with the crowd, but also to provide stylistic information about the repertoire. Audience members are often completely in the dark: they don't know the repertoire, the composers, the styles—they may not have ever encountered the instruments. Thus, addressing the audience gives the director an opportunity to increase their awareness and their appreciation for what's happening on stage.

When talking to the audience, the director should encourage appropriate popular music audience behavior. For instance, the audience may not understand that in a popular music context, the band expects them to applaud soloists in the course of a tune, rather than to wait until the tune is finished. Remember, entertainment is a primary goal of the steel band, and an audience that is accustomed to only attending formal music performances may need to be "trained" to properly enjoy a steel band performance.

Finally, while we shouldn't rely exclusively on a steel band's novel appeal, we should highlight the colorful and vibrant nature of the music with visual stimuli. Colorful outfits, as opposed to concert black attire, are more suited to a steel band performance. Directors and members alike can contribute creative ideas for spicing up the performance venue, the programs, and other elements of the entire experience we call a "performance." Of course, our first goal is to present quality music, but all kinds of musicians and ensembles effectively use elements of performance practice to enhance the experience of witnessing live music.

CLOSING THOUGHTS

In the end, performing is what music is all about. It's what draws most of us into the world of music in the first place. One of the best things about being a steel band director is playing pan or in the engine room as part of the ensemble—we get to be part of the band, rather than simply being in charge of it. While playing in a band keeps us energized, it also puts us in tune with the challenges and rewards that our members experience. Enjoy to the fullest this wonderful aspect of directing your steel band, and have fun!

I must emphasize once again the value of interacting with master performers, composers and arrangers, and teachers from the steel band realm. Either invite them to work personally with your program, or make an effort to see them at clinics, festivals, or workshop events. Nothing can substitute for personal interaction, especially in a musical idiom that stems from an oral tradition, like pan does. Besides, pan is a relatively young endeavor, and it is still developing and changing rapidly. Staying in touch with others in pan is the best way to keep current.

Remember to continuously educate yourself, your members, and your audiences. As musicians, we must always strive to create new fans of what we do—fans who not only enjoy listening to our music, but who can appreciate our art form. Those are the folks who patronize our efforts time and again; they return because they recognize quality, and because they expect it.

Finally, don't just do steel band. Do it well. Though it's not a one-stop repository, this book is, I hope, a resource that you will turn to often as you lead your band.

Good luck, and all the best!

Appendix A

SUGGESTED READING

I have divided the entries here into two categories, pan readings and engine room readings. Pan readings deal with pan itself: the history of the instrument, arranging techniques for steel band, and the like. Engine room readings provide stylistic information for various Latin American and Caribbean grooves you might need to coach.

PAN READINGS

One of the best books about the Trinidadian music-culture is Shannon Dudley's recent offering, *Carnival Music in Trinidad* (Oxford University Press, 2004). Part of the Global Music Series, this text is comprehensive yet brief, detailed but easy to read. The book covers everything from the origins of Carnival and calypso music to the current pop music scene in Trinidad. Included are two entire chapters devoted to pan. Most importantly, an accompanying CD allows the reader to hear exactly what Dudley writes about.

For a more in-depth book on the steel band, try Stephen Stuempfle's *The Steelband Movement* (University of Pennsylvania

Press, 1995). Stuempfle's book is longer than Dudley's, much more scholarly in tone, and has an enormous bibliography and copious endnotes. Stuempfle fills the book with anecdotes and quotations from famous panmen as well as cultural observers in a detailed exposition of the origins and development of the Trinidadian steel band. A more complete treatment of the topic is hard to find.

In the realm of articles, interested readers should check back issues of *Percussive Notes*, the bimonthly journal of the Percussive Arts Society. Over the years, a number of articles dealing with pan history, pedagogy, and people have graced the pages of the journal. A few notables are Tom Miller's article "Steel Drum 101: A Guide to the First Year" (volume 24, no. 4, April 1986); Robert Chappell's profile of pan builder, performer, composer and educator Cliff Alexis titled "Cliff Alexis: Pan Education" (volume 35, no. 3, June 1997); and Jeannine Remy's article "The Steel Band in Trinidad and Tobago: An Overview" (volume 30, no. 4, April 1992). This last one does a great job at boiling down the history of pan into a few pages, and is a very accessible read for high school–aged band members.

Finally, Jeffrey Ross Thomas's entry "Steel Band/Pan" in the reference source *Encyclopedia of Percussion*, edited by John Beck (Garland Press, 1995), is an excellent read. The entry is very detailed, comprehensive, and well-written. Thomas is also the author of *Forty Years of Steel: An Annotated Discography of Steel Band and Pan Recordings, 1951–1991* (Greenwood Press, 1992). Only true "panphiles" would be interested in this last work.

ENGINE ROOM READINGS

As I have already stated a number of times, it is imperative that steel band directors become familiar with the stylistic demands of the repertoire they pursue. To that end, several sources are worth mention. For insight into Afro-Cuban styles of music, readers should consider Frank Malabe and Bob Weiner's *Afro-Cuban Rhythms for Drumset* (Manhattan Music, 1994), which comes with an accompanying CD. Even though it is a drumset book, it nonetheless takes the time to explain the "folkloric" nature of each groove, providing examples of what the conga drums might play in a montuno, for instance. The publisher, Manhattan Music, also offers a comparable book on Brazilian styles titled *Brazilian Rhythms for Drumset* (1993), authored by Duduka de Fonseca and Bob Weiner.

Another author to check out is Ed Uribe. His books, *The Essence of Afro-Cuban Percussion and Drumset* and *The Essence of Brazilian Percussion and Drumset* (Warner Brothers Publications, 1996, 1994), provide very detailed stylistic information on both Afro-Cuban and Brazilian grooves, respectively. These books are extensive, and they also include accompanying recordings of examples.

Lastly, readers may want to consider *Pan Rhythm* by Phil Hawkins (P. Note Publications, n.d.), which primarily contains useful rhythmic exercises, and the end of the book addresses drumset and percussion patterns for calypso and soca.

Appendix B

SUGGESTED LISTENING

This list represents just a small sampling of the many pan recordings available. The entries are divided into three categories: historical interest recordings, steel band recordings, and solo artist/small group recordings. Each category lists annotated entries in alphabetical order by the artist or band name.

You can obtain most of these titles in the United States through either Panyard, Inc. (www.panyard.com) or Pan Ramajay Productions (www.ramajay.com). Recordings in the historical interest section, however, are more difficult to find. Check for these in library collections, or look to order them through large music outlets such as Borders Books and Music or Tower Records. Those interested in early recordings of both pan and calypso should visit the website of Smithsonian-Folkways recordings (www.folkways.si.edu), perhaps the best resource for such music.

HISTORICAL INTEREST RECORDINGS

Westland Steel Band. *The Sound of the Sun*. Nonesuch: H 72016, 1967.

This recording is a good example of an old-time pan sound, prior to the development of modern pan tuning techniques.

Various artists. *The Music of Trinidad.* National Geographic Society, 1971.

Two recordings of Panorama steel bands appear on this recording, along with many other items. The album is a musical snapshot of Carnival in Trinidad in 1971.

STEEL BAND RECORDINGS

Chabot Panhandlers. *Three.* Ramajay Records: RR70007-2, 2002.

The Panhandlers (now affiliated with the College of San Mateo in California) consistently produce high-quality recordings: they are produced well, feature great music, and it is evident that the ensemble is capably coached.

Miami University Steel Band. *Simple Pleasures.* Ramajay Records: RR70014, 2006.

This third offering from the Miami Univeristy Steel Band comprises eight selections from five different American composers of steel band music: Phil Hawkins, Alan Lightner, Tom Miller, Andy Narell, and Chris Tanner.

Andy Narell and Calypsociation. *The Passage.* Heads Up, International: HUCD3086, 2004.

Andy Narell's recording with this Paris, France–based ensemble is perhaps the finest example of a steel band recording to date, especially in terms of production value. Three established jazz horn soloists, Michael Brecker, Paquito D'Rivera, and Hugh Masekela, also appear on the disc. This one is a must-have.

Various artists. *A Panyard Anthology.* Sanch Electronix Limited: Sanch CD 0205-2, 2002.

This two-disc set features twelve total arrangements performed by some of the top steel bands in Trinidad.

Various artists. *Pan Is Beautiful V World Steelband Festival, Volume 2.* Multimedia, Ltd.: PBV 02/88, 1988.

Ever wonder what Gershwin's *Rhapsody in Blue* or Tchaikovsky's *Capriccio Italien* might sound like on pan? Well, get this disc and find out! The World Steelband Festival (known as *Pan Is Beautiful* up to 2000) traditionally features bands performing transcriptions of Western art music classics. Recorded live.

Various artists. *Portraits in Steel: Steelbands of Trinidad and Tobago.* Sanch Electronix Limited: Sanch CD 9701, 1997.

This disc features several important Trinidadian ensembles, including Phase Two, Renegades, and Exodus. There are only five arrangements on the recording (Jit Samaroo's arrangement of Kitchener's *Guitar Pan* is performed twice, at different tempi), but all are done by top Panorama arrangers.

Various artists. *Steelbands of Trinidad and Tobago.* Delos: DE 4015, 1993.

Another compilation of Panorama music, this disc from the early 1990s comprises eight arrangements from various composers, including Len "Boogsie" Sharpe, Jit Samaroo, and Ken "Professor" Philmore.

Various artists. *Steelbands of Trinidad and Tobago in Tribute to Ray Holman.* Delos: DE 4025, 1994.

Ray Holman's arrangements for Panorama are nothing short of classic. Every steel band director should know the sound of Ray's music, and this disc provides nearly 74 minutes of it.

SOLO ARTIST/SMALL GROUP RECORDINGS

Gary Gibson. *Yahboy!* GPG10505, 2005.

Gary Gibson plays lead pan, whereas most solo pan artists use the double second pan as their primary instrument. Gibson is also an accomplished composer, and this disc features fantastic music in a wide variety of styles. The band backing him up is top notch.

Phil Hawkins. *H2O.* Ramajay Records: RR70013, 2005.

H2O is Hawkins' first major release. In the steel band world he is perhaps best known for his steel band arrangements, many of which are accessible to beginner-level ensembles. With this recording, Hawkins demonstrates that he is equally adept at fronting a band.

Ray Holman. *In Touch.* Ramajay Records: RR70009-2, 2003.

Aside from being in demand as a Panorama arranger, Ray Holman has a fine reputation as a performer and soloist. This disc showcases his compositions in a combo setting. Fake book-style arrangements of the tunes on this disc are available through Pan Ramajay Productions.

Andy Narell. *Behind the Bridge*. Heads Up, International: HUCD3047, 1998.

Actually, *any* recording from Andy Narell is worth owning. I have only highlighted this one because it is both recent and unusual in the sense that Narell does not employ his standard backup band instrumentation. An additional treat is Narell's solo realization of David Rudder's *Nuff Respect*. You won't believe that only one man is capable of playing melody and accompaniment on a single set of pans the way that Narell does.

Panoramic (featuring Liam Teague). *Panoramic*. Rhythmic Union Records: RU4868, 2005.

If you have not yet heard Liam Teague play, get this disc immediately. Teague is perhaps best known for having some of the fastest hands in the pan world, but this recording clearly shows his high level of musicianship and his ability to navigate challenging chord changes with ease. The ensemble, featuring Teague's colleague at NIU, marimbist Robert Chappell, is excellent.

Pan Ramajay. *Back for More*. Ramajay Records: RR 004, 2000.

Pan Ramajay has at its heart three Bay Area pan artists—Tom Miller, Alan Lightner, and Jim Munzenrider. The recording includes music by Ray Holman and Darren Dyke, and features an all-star rhythm section: Paul van Wageningen on drums, Nelson Braxton on bass, and Michael Spiro on percussion.

Sakésho (featuring Andy Narell). *Sakésho*. Heads Up, International: HUCD3069, 2002.

This quartet featuring Narell as the frontman produces some absolutely stunning music. While many of the pieces are based in Caribbean musical styles, this is a jazz record to be sure.

Appendix C

SUGGESTED RESOURCES

SHEET MUSIC

The following steel band sheet music publishers devote their entire catalog to pan music.

Coyle Steel Drums
www.coyledrums.com
(850) 475-8930

> Coyle Steel Drums began publishing steel band music a few years ago. Their catalog is somewhat limited, offering charts from only a small range of composers. There are some notables, however: for a change of pace in your programming, try a heavy metal–style tune from Tracy Thornton.

Hillbridge Music
www.hillbridge.com
(412) 221-0678 or (503) 324-0326

> The Hillbridge catalog has diverse offerings from a number of composers and arrangers. Arrangements, as opposed to original compositions, dominate the catalog. A number of arrangements

feature vocalists and horn soloists, as well as adaptations of wind band arrangements (one of the owners of Hillbridge, Marc Svaline, led a highly successful high school steel band program for many years).

Panyard, Inc.
www.panyard.com
(800) 377-0202

Panyard has a broad catalog that represents various styles, including classical music transcriptions. They also offer a number of solo pieces for lead, double second, and guitar/cello pan. One of the best features of Panyard's catalog is the presence of transcriptions from Trinidad's annual Panorama competition. For some folks, these transcriptions represent the greatest music in the idiom, and some of the best composers of Panorama music are represented. Panyard's catalog grades all pieces according to difficulty, which is helpful for those unfamiliar with the repertoire.

Pan Press
www.panpress.com
(630) 587-3473

The Pan Press catalog almost exclusively features original compositions for steel band by owner Paul Ross. Despite the absence of composer diversity, there is a nice balance between easy, moderate, and difficult charts. Also, Pan Press carries solos for lead pan, double second pan, and guitar pan, including a few compositions by renowned composer-performer Liam Teague. These solos are appropriate for pan players in high school or college.

Pan Ramajay Productions
www.ramajay.com
(510) 451-3268

Pan Ramajay Productions focuses nearly exclusively on original music for steel band, and publishes a limited slate of composers.

Most of these are at the top of the steel band realm, including Ray Holman, Tom Miller, Andy Narell, and Len "Boogsie" Sharpe. The catalog is balanced not only in terms of difficulty level, but also in terms of musical style.

The following companies publish percussion ensemble music, but also offer a limited number of pan titles.

C. Alan Publications
www.c-alanpublications.com
(336) 272-3920
    C. Alan Publications carries only a few steel band charts. However, it is worth noting that many of these are written for beginner-level ensembles.

drop6media
www.drop6.com
(877) 773-7676
    This catalog contains only a few pan titles; some are arrangements (including transcriptions of orchestral music) and some are original compositions. All pieces are graded according to difficulty, and most of the steel band titles are fairly difficult. Because drop6 caters primarily to percussion ensembles, the steel band charts are written in such a way as to allow instrument substitutions (such as substituting marimba or vibes for pan parts).

CONFERENCES AND WORKSHOPS

International Association of Pan Enthusiasts Annual Convention
www.panenthusiast.org
(330) 745-3837
    IAPE is a newly formed organization (2005) dedicated to "the Development, Support and Promotion of the Steel Drum art

form, its history, instruments and music." The association's annual convention, typically held in April, features a festival competition for bands, clinics and performances by pan artists and educators, and vendor displays.

Mannette Steel Drums, Ltd. "Festival of Steel"
www.mannettesteeldrums.com
(866) 237-3786
Held annually in July in Morgantown, West Virginia, the "Festival of Steel" is perhaps the most comprehensive workshop devoted to steel band in the United States. Attendees spend most of the day playing in a steel band (personnel are slotted according to ability/experience), coached by various prestigious pan artists. Hands-on clinics, demonstrations, and artist performances round out the schedule.

MENC
www.menc.org
(800) 336-3768
MENC, the nation's premier association for music educators, offers a national conference every two years, and divisional (regional) conferences annually. It's always a good idea to check the upcoming conference programs for steel band topics or presenters. Also be sure to check your state music education organization's conference program each year.

Percussive Arts Society International Convention
www.pas.org
(580) 353-1455
PASIC is an annual convention that brings together the top names in all fields of percussion. The "world" element is always well represented, so it is worth checking the conference schedule annually to see if any pan groups or artists are featured. PASIC is typically held in early to mid-November in a Midwestern city.

ABOUT THE AUTHOR

Chris Tanner, D.M.A., is assistant professor of music at Miami University. He first became interested in world music as an undergraduate student at West Virginia University, where he studied African percussion with Phil Faini and was a founding member of the WVU Steel Band. While at WVU, he also met and worked with Ellie Mannette, an internationally recognized leader in the steel band world.

While pursuing his master's degree at Miami University in the early 1990s, Tanner founded the Miami University Steel Band. The ensemble has grown into one of the most active and recognized steel bands in the United States. Tanner is active as a performer, educator, and composer/arranger. He has served as a guest clinician or performing artist at numerous festivals, workshops, high schools, and universities. He is a seven-time commissioned composer/arranger, and his works are published through both Pan Ramajay Productions and Panyard, Inc. His compositions can be heard on the Miami University Steel Band's three compact disc releases, produced and distributed by Pan Ramajay Productions: *Simple Pleasures* (2006), *One More Soca* (2003), and *Burnin'* (2001).